W9-CKL-305

WILD
BOUNTY

Game Feasts, Outdoor Flavors

By Jim and Ann Casada

MINNETONKA, MINNESOTA

About the Authors

South Carolinians Ann and Jim Casada grew up in households where wild bounty figured prominently in daily fare, and that has continued to be the case in their life together. They are the authors of an earlier work on game cooking, *The Complete Venison Cookbook*, and have been major contributors to several volumes on game cooking. Also, Jim edited *From Campsite to Kitchen: Tastes and Traditions of America's Great Outdoors*, for the Outdoor Writer's Association of America (OWAA). A full-time freelance outdoor writer, Jim currently serves as the president of OWAA. In addition to his joint efforts with Ann on this and other game and fish cookbooks, he has written or edited more than 20 books, including the award-winning *Modern Fly Fishing* published by the North American Fishing Club. Both Jim and Ann are avid outdoor enthusiasts who enjoy living close to nature, savoring the products of the good earth, and sharing that *Wild Bounty* with readers like you.

✦ ✦ ✦ ✦ ✦ ✦ ✦ ✦ ✦

Wild Bounty
Game Feasts, Outdoor Flavors

Tom Carpenter
Director of Book Development

Dan Kennedy
Book Production Manager

Jennifer Guinea, Heather Koshiol
Book Development Coordinators

Becky Landes
Book Design and Production

Phil Aarrestad
Commissioned Photography/Design Coordinator

Ron Essex
Assistant Photographer

Robin Krause
Food Stylist

Susan Hammes, Susan Telleen, Genie Zarling
Assistant Food Stylists

Special Thanks To:
Cabin Fever Sports
Doug Beasley, Vision Quest
East Bay Sugarbush Syrup
Radde Taxidermy
Talking Elk Farm
Thomas Aarrestad Illustrations

PHOTO CREDITS
Phil Aarrestad: All Sidebars, 8–9, 46–47, 62–63, 70, 76, 78–79, 83, 94–95, 100, 102–103, 106–107, 120–121, 145, 146, 155. Grady Allen: 17, 47, 59. Lance Beeny: 79, 127. Chuck Carpenter: 110, 125. Tom Carpenter: 152. Jim Casada: 10, 50, 57, 61, 72, 111, 121, 123, 128, 132, 133, 134, 137, 140, 149, 153. John R. Ford: 9, 44, 101, 135. Michael H. Francis: 113. Bill Kinney: 34, 41. Bill Marchel: 39, 84, 86, 88, 141. Wyman Meinzer: 71. Soc Clay Inc.: 66, 114, 142, 148. Ron Spomer: 7, 29, 43, 91, 107, 151, 154. Dusan Smetana, THE GREEN AGENCY: 24.

3 4 5 6 7 8 / 03 02 01

ISBN 1-58159-104-7

North American Hunting Club
12301 Whitewater Drive
Minnetonka, MN 55343
www.huntingclub.com

TABLE OF CONTENTS

ACKNOWLEDGMENTS

One of the enduring joys of being closely connected to the outdoors is sharing experiences with others of a similar turn of mind. Tales tall and true, campfire chats, reliving hunts past and planning those yet to come, family outings to pick berries or gather nuts, and related activities … all loom large in this process of caring and sharing. Yet to our way of thinking, there is nothing that quite compares with exchanging, sampling and savoring recipes from nature's larder. Whatever the occasion and wherever the place, be it a rustic back country camp or a holiday dining table set with the finest crystal and silver, game and other wild foods are truly special. They become even more so when family and friends are involved.

Such is the case with *Wild Bounty*. We owe debts of gratitude not only to the individuals named below but to all those who have enriched our lives over the years as we partook of dishes and delicacies offered up by the natural world. First and foremost, we must thank those who nurtured us and served as mentors in shaping our ongoing love affair with the wild world. Grandpa Joe Casada kept a shining spark in a wonderstruck lad's eyes with his storytelling of hunts that took place late in the 19th century, and Commodore Casada gave me that most precious of gifts, a love of hunting. Ernest Fox shared his passions for the field with Ann, his only daughter, and both our mothers, Lucy Fox and Anna Lou Casada, knew well how to handle nature's treasure trove in the kitchen.

To those who provided recipes or offered helpful tips, we are deeply appreciative. They include Judy Lyon, George Mayfield, Rick Snipes, Nancy Davidson, Frankie Ledford, Kaye Upgren, Ruth Buckley, Steve and Denise Wagner, Gail Wright, Elaine Tanner and Etah Kirkpatrick. Our daughter and son-in-law, Natasha and Eric Getway, contributed both through encouragement and through their own budding apprenticeship in the wonderful world of game cookery.

Any book involves input and effort by individuals other than the authors, and certainly such is the case with the present work. We owe much to the efforts of Tom Carpenter, Heather Koshiol, Jen Guinea and their colleagues in the Book Department at the North American Hunting Club. Their guidance and encouragement are solid foundations underlying the conception, preparation and ultimate completion of this book.

Finally, we are both appreciative of just how many truly good and gracious people earn their livelihood, as we do, from connections with the outdoors. To these friends and members of the South Carolina Outdoor Press Association, the Southeastern Outdoor Press Association, the Outdoor Writers Association of America, we express our thanks, and the same applies to those in the outdoor industry in general. We bow in gratitude for what they mean to us not merely from the perspective of this book but in our lives.

—*Jim and Ann Casada*

FOREWORD

Game cookbooks come in many forms.

One category is, "Nice to look at, but I could never make that stuff." These are your fancy-schmancy books from chefs who might cook a little game farm venison, elk or duck in their restaurant and think they know game cooking. But who has the time–or French cooking school degree–needed to make the stuff?

Another category is, "Doesn't look so great, but of all those recipes, which ones should I chance my hard-earned game on?" These are your down-and-dirty books that are put together quickly from the crumpled files of a bunch of contributors, and look the part. There are certainly some recipe gems, but how do you find them?

So leave it to your Club to come along and pull it all together–proven recipes you *can* create, every one guaranteed to do your game proud on the table … and beautiful pages too.

We found two of the best game cooks we know, Jim and Ann Casada, to write *Wild Bounty–Game Feasts, Outdoor Flavors* for you. Jim and Ann provide an unmatched combination–vast outdoor knowledge and a deep understanding of game meat's special needs–to every recipe. Most of these ideas are simple, some a little more involved, but they all allow your *Wild Bounty*, the game, to be king.

You'll also find the bonus of the Casadas' insights on other wild and natural foods–in many of the game recipes, as well as other recipes that use nature's harvest. You can glean some of this other harvest (nuts, berries, fruits and more) while hunting; for others, you'll have to hit the great outdoors at other times of the year; tough duty!

I wish Jim Casada could talk you through some of these recipes, like he did for me. You could hear his southern voice and feel in it his love for the game, cooking it and eating it.

One day I plan on hunting turkeys with this son of the South, because his skills in the woods are as great as those he and Ann share in the kitchen. Maybe he'll help me call up a gobbler, but when we're not in the woods I am going to talk him into creating some of these game meals. Until then, I'm lucky to have the recipes and knowledge imparted in the pages that follow. So are you.

Enjoy your *Wild Bounty*!

Tom Carpenter
Editor–North American Hunting Club Books

INTRODUCTION

Archibald Rutledge, one of America's great hunters of yesteryear and an individual who wrote close to 50 books on the outdoors, once observed that there was "much more to hunting than hunting." Among the benefits he enumerated were "renewed health, a more wholesome outlook on life, [and] a reverence for the miracle of creation." Old Flintlock, as he was known to family and close friends, reckoned that there was something inherently American in the expression, "shoot straight," and that the "privilege of hunting was about as fine a heritage as we have." He believed that "hunting gives a man a sense of balance, sanity, and a comprehension of the true values of life."

Countless other writers of note, from President Theodore Roosevelt and Nobel Laureate William Faulkner to the man who was perhaps our finest sporting scribe, Robert Ruark, have praised the virtues of hunting. A common thread running through the bright fabric of their work and that of other notables in the field focuses on the pleasure of splendid repasts coming from the hunt. For example, Nash Buckingham, who is today a virtual cult figure among quail hunters and waterfowlers, wrote so well on the joys of game feasts that he literally can start the reader's salivary glands flowing in some of the stories found in books like *The Shootinest Gent'man* and *Hallowed Years*. Anyone who reads timeless tales in Ruark's *The Old Man and the Boy* such as "Terrapin Stew Costs Ten Bucks a Quart" or "Mister Howard Was a Real Gent" soon arrives at the inescapable conclusion that game provides as fine a fare as any human could wish. Similarly, Rutledge's readers discover that no Southern holiday table was deemed fully set without being graced by a haunch of venison or a wild turkey, with platters of quail, ducks and doves flanking the festive centerpiece.

The point these writers and others of their ilk made, and made consistently, was that consuming the results of a successful trip afield was part and parcel of the hunting experience. Sound sporting ethics demanded that the hunter ate what he killed, while common sense dictated that to do otherwise would not only be wrong-headed but a missed opportunity for dining delight. This book is written from precisely that perspective. We hunt for pleasure and the pure joy of seeking oneness with the wild world, and as we do so it is with full recognition of the fact that one of the most enjoyable parts of the process is cooking and consuming game.

In the pages that follow we devote six chapters to sharing scores of game recipes that have filled and fulfilled us. There is also a concluding chapter devoted to another part of nature's bounty—the nuts, berries, fruits and vegetables that grow in the wild. These foods form logical and luscious companions to game, and it is our belief that you will find that the process of procuring them blends beautifully with both your hunting and culinary experiences. Each chapter concludes with a selection of complete menus, and one of the features of these menus is the inclusion of dishes that feature wild foods. A number of these complimentary wild food dishes are marked with an asterisk, which means that the recipe will be found in the chapter "Feasts and Flavors from Nature's Garden." Interspersed throughout the book you will find tips and comments intended to simplify matters or add zest to your game cooking, and many of the individual recipes include hints that users might find helpful.

Cooking wild game need not be a daunting or complicated task. With game in hand, along with a basic understanding of how to make and use marinades, some simple utensils, and use of stove top, oven or grill, you are ready to get down to the rewarding business of cooking. Game cookery, contrary to the impressions of many, also need not be particularly restricted in terms of the types of dishes offered. While the recipes found here range widely in terms of complexity, the majority are simple, straight-forward approaches to game preparation. We firmly believe that any truly useful and user-friendly game cookbook should offer culinary road maps to fine eating that the average person can readily follow, and such is our goal in the scores of recipes given in *Wild Bounty*. Happy hunting and *bon appétit!*

— *Jim Casada*

VENISON

Venison figured prominently in human diet long before the first Europeans set foot on American soil, and the meat continued to be a staple food item until late in the 19th century. Incidentally, in the context of venison as a foodstuff, it should be noted at the outset that the word "venison" applies not only to whitetails but to any ungulate or, in Webster's words, "animal of the deer kind." That consideration should be kept in mind when preparing these recipes. In most cases the recipe will work just as well for elk, mule deer, pronghorn or moose meat as for that of the whitetail; and when ground venison or stew meat is involved, such is virtually always the case. In other words, while most of what follows in this chapter focuses specifically on whitetails, users of the cookbook should not consider this a limiting factor if they happen to be fortunate enough to have other big game in the larder.

While the deer in particular meant vital sustenance for pioneers, along with the occasional welcome break from everyday drudgery to hunt, there was a great deal of prodigality associated with early hunting of the animal. So much was this the case, in fact, that the combination of market hunting, poor conservation practices, no seasons or limits and related factors led to a dramatic decline in whitetail numbers. Indeed, in the first half of the 20th century precious few

Americans, sportsmen or not, knew the joys of eating venison. All of that has changed over the last two generations, thanks to one of the century's great wildlife comeback sagas. Today white-tail numbers are at record highs, and over much of the

nation deer hunting ranks at the top of the list of favored hunting pursuits.

Almost 90 percent of the country's population lives within reasonable driving distance of places where whitetails can be hunted with quite realistic expectations of success. Furthermore, hunting has proven to be a vital management tool, and as deer numbers continue to soar, longer seasons and more liberal limits are the word of the day. Fortunately, venison is as tasty as the animal is abundant, and the size of a deer is such that the hunter who manages to put a deer or two in his freezer each fall has the makings of scores of meals for the coming months.

"Bringing home the bacon" in the form of a nice deer leads to a real sense of accomplishment, and making full and proper use of the meat completes the cycle of ethical sportsmanship that every hunter should practice. Enjoying the benefits of this marvelous game animal ends on the table, but the whole process is exceptionally fulfilling.

LEMON VENISON STEAK

4 slices bacon
1/2 large onion, chopped
1 tablespoon sugar
10 (1-inch-thick) venison steak cutlets from backstrap
Juice of 1 lemon
Lemon pepper

Fry bacon in a cast iron skillet. Remove slices from the pan, leaving 2 tablespoons drippings in skillet and reserving remaining drippings. Add onion to drippings and sprinkle with sugar; cook until onion is tender. Remove onion and return reserved drippings to the skillet. Place cutlets in the skillet; squeeze a small amount of lemon juice on each cutlet and season with lemon pepper. Cook quickly; meat is best if cutlets are still slightly pink in the center. Add crumbled bacon and onion to cutlets and reheat. Serve immediately with wild rice.

SERVES 3 - 4

LOIN STEAKS WITH RASPBERRY SAUCE

1 pound loin steaks
1/3 cup Dale's steak seasoning
1/3 cup water
1/2 stick margarine
1 garlic clove, minced
1/2 cup raspberry jam

Marinate loin in Dale's steak seasoning and water, drain. Melt the margarine and add garlic. Sauté briefly. Add loin and cook to desired doneness. Remove loin and de-glaze pan with jam. Serve as sauce for dipping loin.

Wild black raspberries ripening and inviting the visiting picker.

Shrimp-Stuffed Tenderloin

SHRIMP-STUFFED TENDERLOIN

   1   *whole venison tenderloin*
¹/₂-1   *cup Italian salad dressing*
  12   *whole shrimp, cooked and peeled*
   1   *teaspoon Old Bay*
   1   *tablespoon butter, melted*
   2   *teaspoons lemon juice*
  1-2   *slices bacon*

Cut loin lengthwise to within ¹/₄ - ¹/₂ inch of bottom to butterfly. Place loin in Italian dressing to marinate for at least 4 hours. Cook shrimp in water seasoned to taste with Old Bay and peel. Place shrimp end to end inside loin. Melt butter in microwave and add lemon juice; drizzle over shrimp. Close meat around shrimp and secure with toothpicks (or string). Place bacon strips over shrimp and secure with toothpicks. Place loin on a rack in broiler pan and roast at 400°F for about 40 minutes or until rare. (An instant-read meat thermometer is very helpful here.) Meanwhile, prepare Wine Sauce.

WINE SAUCE

¹/₂   *cup butter (the real thing)*
¹/₄   *cup finely chopped onion*
¹/₂   *cup sliced mushrooms*
1-2   *large garlic cloves, minced*
¹/₂   *cup white wine*
¹/₂   *teaspoon Worcestershire sauce*

Melt butter. Sauté onion, mushrooms and garlic until tender. Add wine and Worcestershire sauce and simmer slowly to reduce to about half. To serve, slice loin, remove toothpicks, and spoon on wine sauce.

Tip: Serve with baked brown rice and baked apricots; both can be placed in the oven while the roast cooks. Add a green salad and you have a delicious meal.

TIPS ON CLEANING AND PROCESSING

Two of the most common reasons for inferior or poor-tasting venison are improper cleaning and processing. Whether you live in bitterly cold climates or the sunny South, you should field dress your deer as soon as it is retrieved. Moreover, once the entrails have been removed, a stick or similar means should be employed to keep the body cavity open. This lets the meat cool down more quickly. For gut-shot animals, be sure to clean away every vestige of stomach contents, and no matter where the shot hits, trim away bloody bits and bone fragments.

Processing venison is a fine art and one that is seldom practiced in proper fashion. Understandably, commercial processors are anxious to follow a rapid turn-around approach which means "meat in, meat out." Yet for the finest in taste and tenderness, venison should be aged in a cooler for a week to 10 days at temperatures within a degree or two of 38°F. Ideally, the hide should be left intact during the aging process, although seeking a processor willing to do this often can be an exercise in futility. At the very least, insist on several days of aging.

VENISON TENDERLOIN WITH TOMATO BASIL SAUCE

4	venison loin steaks
3	tablespoons butter or margarine, divided
2	tablespoons olive oil
1/2	cup minced vidalia onion
1	garlic clove, minced
1/2	cup red wine
1	cup mushrooms, thinly sliced
1/2	cup heavy cream (skim milk can be used)
1	medium tomato, peeled and coarsely chopped
4	large fresh basil leaves, chopped
1/4	teaspoon salt
1 1/2	teaspoons coarsely ground black pepper

Pat steaks dry. Rub pepper onto both sides of each steak.

In large heavy skillet, melt 2 tablespoons butter and olive oil over high heat. Add steaks and cook until browned and to desired doneness. Transfer steaks to warmed dish and loosely cover with foil to keep warm.

Add remaining 1 tablespoon butter to skillet. Add onion and garlic and sauté for 1 minute. Add wine to skillet and heat to boiling, stirring to scrape up any browned bits. Add mushrooms and cook, stirring frequently until softened, for about 3 minutes. Add cream, tomato and basil and simmer until mixture begins to thicken for about 1 minute. Season with salt and pepper. Spoon sauce over steaks and serve.

SERVES 4

Venison Loin Medallions with Cherry Sauce

VENISON LOIN MEDALLIONS WITH CHERRY SAUCE

1 cup low-salt chicken stock or broth
1 cup beef broth
½ cup cherry liqueur
⅓ cup red ruby cherry pie filling
1 tablespoon cornstarch dissolved in ¼ cup water
3 tablespoons butter, divided
8 venison loin steak medallions
    (about ½ inch thick)

Combine chicken stock and beef broth in small, heavy saucepan. Boil until liquid is reduced to 1 cup (about 15 minutes). Add cherry liqueur and boil until liquid is reduced to ¾ cup (about 5 minutes). Whisk in cherry pie filling and simmer until sauce starts to thicken. Add cornstarch dissolved in water and stir until sauce thickens. Whisk in 1 tablespoon of the butter. Season sauce with salt and pepper if desired. Set aside.

Sprinkle venison with salt and pepper. Melt remaining 2 tablespoons of the butter in a large non-stick skillet over medium-high heat. Add venison to skillet and cook to desired doneness. Place 2 medallions on each plate and top with cherry sauce.

Serves 4

Venison

Blueberry Backstrap

BLUEBERRY BACKSTRAP

2 tablespoons butter, melted
4 venison loin steaks, cut ¹/₂ inch thick
  Juice and peel of one large fresh lemon
    (about 2 tablespoons)
1 cup chicken broth
4 tablespoons butter
1 cup fresh blueberries
  Several generous dashes ground cinnamon
  Several dashes ground ginger
  Salt and freshly ground black pepper to taste

Melt 2 tablespoons butter in large skillet and cook venison loin steaks until medium-rare and browned on both sides. Place on platter and keep warm. De-glaze skillet with lemon juice and peel and chicken broth. Cook over high heat to reduce liquid to about ¹/₂ cup. Lower heat to medium and add 4 tablespoons butter, whisking one tablespoon in at a time. Add blueberries, cinnamon, ginger, salt and pepper. Pour blueberry sauce over steaks and serve immediately.

SERVES 4

Tip: Frozen blueberries may be used.

MERLOT LOIN

1 large garlic clove, minced
1 teaspoon freshly ground black pepper
1/2 teaspoon Italian seasoning
2 tablespoons plus 2 teaspoons olive oil
1 venison loin, cut into 1-inch-thick steaks
2 tablespoons butter (the real thing), divided
2 tablespoons chopped onion
1/2 cup sliced mushrooms
1/2 cup beef bouillon
1/4 cup merlot wine
1 teaspoon Worcestershire sauce

Place minced garlic, pepper, Italian seasoning and 2 teaspoons of the olive oil in a bowl and mix well. Rub into loin steaks and refrigerate for 2 - 3 hours.

Pour remaining 2 tablespoons of the olive oil in a skillet and add 1 tablespoon of the butter. Heat to medium high and add steaks. Cook about 4 minutes per side. Do not overcook. Centers of steaks should be pink. Remove steaks from pan and add onion and mushrooms. Sauté briefly and add beef bouillon, merlot wine and Worcestershire sauce. Increase heat to high and reduce liquid by half. Blend in 1 remaining tablespoon of the butter and pour sauce over steaks. Serve immediately.

SERVES 3 - 4

WORCESTERSHIRE STEAKS

3 - 4 venison steaks

MARINADE

1/4 cup Worcestershire sauce
1/4 cup olive oil
2 tablespoons lemon juice
1/2 teaspoon onion salt
1 garlic clove, minced
1/2 teaspoon black pepper

Mix marinade ingredients and place in a sealable plastic bag. Add steaks and marinate for 3 - 4 hours in refrigerator. Grill steaks over hot coals or broil. Do not overcook. About 4 - 5 minutes per side is usually adequate. Serve immediately.

DIJON LOIN STEAKS

BATTER

1/3 cup Dijon mustard
3 tablespoons water
2 teaspoons Worcestershire sauce
1 garlic clove, minced
1/2 teaspoon Italian seasoning

1 cup dry, fine bread crumbs (from whole wheat bread)
1 pound venison loin steaks
2 tablespoons canola oil

Combine all batter ingredients and mix well; place in a shallow dish. Place bread crumbs in second shallow dish. Dip venison loin steaks first in batter to coat, then dredge in bread crumbs. Place canola oil in non-stick skillet and cook steaks over medium-high heat. Cook about 5 minutes or until golden brown on both sides. Do not overcook and turn only once. Steaks should still be pink in the center. Serve immediately.

SERVES 4

ERIC'S SPECIAL STEAK MARINADE

3 - 4 venison steaks

MARINADE

1/4 cup Dale's steak seasoning
1/2 cup water
1 tablespoon Worcestershire sauce
1 tablespoon A-1 Steak Sauce
1/2 tablespoon another steak sauce such as Heinz 57, London Steak Sauce, or Crosse and Blackwell Steak Sauce

Mix ingredients well and marinate venison steaks 3 - 4 hours. Grill to desired doneness and serve immediately. Do not overcook steaks; they should still be pink on the inside.

Tip: The secret is to use different kinds of steak sauces for a blend of flavors.

THE MAGIC OF MARINADES

Venison can be both tough and dry, and these two concerns, along with mention of a "gamey" or "wild" taste, are the most frequently encountered complaints voiced by those who say they do not care for the meat. To a considerable degree all these problems can be rectified by use of marinades, although the problems are sometimes products of overcooking or a mindset which expects venison to taste exactly like beef. Most good game cooks have one or two favorite marinades for venison, but it is fun to experiment with marinades, and in that regard here are some hints you might want to consider.

Buttermilk is an overlooked but effective marinade, either by itself or in combination with other ingredients, which both moistens and tenderizes venison. Much the same is true of grape juice, and it is also worth noting that venison is a meat which lends itself wonderfully well to combinations which feature hearty fruit or berry flavors. Indeed, many of the recipes in this chapter involve such unions of flavors, and it is particularly rewarding to dine on meat from a deer you have shot with accompanying dishes prepared from ingredients you have gathered in the wild.

ELAINE'S ITALIAN VENISON STEAK

2	medium onions, chopped
2	garlic cloves, chopped
2	carrots, chopped
2	ribs celery, chopped
1/2	cup fresh parsley
4	bay leaves
1	teaspoon rosemary
1	teaspoon sage leaves
20	peppercorns
10	whole cloves
1/3	cup vinegar
1/2	cup vegetable oil
1/4	cup Worcestershire sauce
1	cup soy sauce
	Juice of 2 lemons
2	pounds venison steaks
3-4	slices bacon, chopped
1	cup red wine
1	cup beef bouillon
2-3	tablespoons flour

Combine onions, garlic, carrots and celery with parsley, bay leaves, rosemary, sage, peppercorns and cloves. Add vinegar, oil, Worcestershire sauce, soy sauce and lemon juice. Place steaks in non-aluminum container and add vegetable mixture. Cover and refrigerate. Marinate for 3 - 4 days; stir twice daily.

To cook, remove meat and pat dry. Remove vegetables from liquid, reserving marinade. Fry several strips of chopped bacon. Remove bacon; lightly brown steaks in bacon fat. Remove meat; add vegetables to fat and lightly brown. Return meat to pan with vegetables. Add red wine, beef bouillon and marinade liquid. Heat mixture to boiling; reduce heat, cover and simmer for 1 1/2 hours. Remove meat and stir in flour to thicken. Remove bay leaves and return meat to gravy. Serve over hot rice.

PINEAPPLE GARLIC LOIN STEAK WITH MUSHROOM SAUCE

1 whole loin, cut into 1-inch-thick slices

PINEAPPLE MARINADE

1 (6-ounce) can pineapple juice
1 tablespoon teriyaki marinade and sauce
1 garlic clove, minced

Place loin in marinade and refrigerate for 2 - 3 hours. Drain and quickly cook steaks in grilling pan, broil, or on open grill. Cook until slightly pink in the center. Place cooked loin on deep platter and cover with mushroom sauce.

MUSHROOM SAUCE

3 tablespoons butter or margarine
2 garlic cloves, minced
1½ cups sliced fresh mushrooms
¼ teaspoon dried thyme
¼ teaspoon parsley
1 teaspoon cornstarch
1 cup chicken broth
Salt and pepper to taste

Melt butter and cook garlic for about 20 seconds; add mushrooms and sauté until tender. Add herbs. Mix cornstarch and broth and add to mushrooms. Cook until thickened and smooth. Pour over steaks and serve immediately with garlic spaghetti.

LOIN STEAKS WITH CRAB, SHRIMP AND SCALLOP SAUCE

1 tablespoon olive oil
1 tablespoon butter or margarine
1 pound loin steaks, cut ½ inch thick
Salt and pepper to taste

Place olive oil and butter in a large skillet and quickly cook venison loin until medium rare. Keep steaks warm on a platter. It is best to cook loin after sauce has started thickening.

CRAB, SHRIMP AND SCALLOP SAUCE

2 tablespoons olive oil
½ pound fresh mushrooms, sliced
2 cups whipping cream
¼ cup White Zinfandel wine
¼ cup butter, cut into 12 pieces
½ pound crab meat
8-12 medium shrimp, cooked and shelled
6-8 sea scallops, cooked and chopped

Heat olive oil in a large skillet. Add mushrooms and sauté 5 minutes. Add cream and wine and reduce until thickened (about 10 - 12 minutes). Season with salt and pepper. Stir in butter one piece at a time incorporating each piece completely before adding next. Add crab meat, shrimp and scallops; heat through, for about 1 minute. Pour over venison. Serve immediately.

<u>SERVES 4</u>

BOURGUIGNON VENISON

  2 medium onions, peeled and sliced
  2 tablespoons olive oil
  2 pounds venison, cut into 1-inch cubes
1½ tablespoons flour
  ½ teaspoon marjoram
  ½ teaspoon thyme
  ½ teaspoon pepper
  1 (10½-ounce) can beef consommé
  1 (10½-ounce) can beef broth, double strength
  1 cup burgundy (or other hearty red wine)
  1 jar sliced mushrooms or ¾ pound fresh mushrooms
    Salt to taste (may not need because of salt in
      canned broths)

Sauté onions in olive oil in Dutch oven until translucent; remove onions and set aside. Add venison to Dutch oven and cook, adding a bit more olive oil if necessary. When browned well on all sides, sprinkle flour, marjoram, thyme and pepper over venison. Stir for about 1 minute to coat venison well and cook flour. Then add consommé, broth and burgundy and stir. Simmer very slowly for about 3 - 3½ hours until venison is tender. Allow to cook down for intense flavor. More consommé and wine may be added if needed. After cooking, return onions to Dutch oven and add mushrooms. Stir well and simmer another hour. The sauce should be thick and dark brown. Serve with a wild and white rice mixture, roasted asparagus, garlic bread sticks and burgundy.

SERVES 8 - 10

GRILLED LOIN STEAKS

1 venison loin

MARINADE

1 cup low-sodium soy sauce
1 large garlic clove, minced
1 tablespoon honey
1 tablespoon steak sauce (your choice)
  Several dashes Tabasco sauce

Cut loin into 1-inch-thick steaks. Place in a resealable plastic bag. Mix marinade ingredients well and pour into the bag over steaks. Marinate in refrigerator 3 - 4 hours. Place on grill or use grilling pan and cook on medium high to desired doneness. Do not overcook.

Tip: Do not have the heat too high or the marinade will burn on the exterior of the steaks. The touch of honey adds a great deal to the flavor but does tend to burn if the heat is high. Baked apricots make a wonderful accompaniment to these steaks. Try them with duck or quail also.

BAKED APRICOTS

  1 (16-ounce) can apricot halves, drained
15 Ritz crackers, crushed
  2 tablespoons light brown sugar
  2 tablespoons butter, melted

Place drained apricots in a casserole dish. Roll crackers into crumbs. Sprinkle crackers on top of apricots. Sprinkle brown sugar over crackers. Pour melted butter over top. Bake at 350°F about 15 - 20 minutes or until hot, bubbly and golden brown.

SERVES 2

Tip: If you wish to make a larger casserole, alternate layers of apricots, crumbs and brown sugar.

Grilled Loin Steaks with Marinade

Venison

Loin Steaks with Apricot Mustard Sauce

LOIN STEAKS WITH APRICOT MUSTARD SAUCE

4-6 *venison loin steaks*
Salt
Black pepper
Butter

APRICOT MUSTARD SAUCE

1/2 *cup grainy brown mustard*
1/3 *cup apricot jam*
1/4 *cup brandy*

Heat a non-stick skillet over medium-high heat; sprinkle the skillet lightly with salt and add steak. Cook until browned and turn steak (sprinkling the pan with salt again before placing back in pan). Cook until steak reaches desired doneness (do not overcook) and sprinkle with freshly ground black pepper. Top steak with a small pat of butter and allow to melt into steak before removing from the pan.

While steaks are cooking, heat mustard, jam and brandy in a small saucepan over medium heat, stirring frequently, until jam has melted and ingredients are well combined. Drizzle sauce over steaks and serve immediately.

<u>SERVES 4</u>

PEPPER STEAK

1/2 cup soy sauce
1 teaspoon sugar
1 garlic clove, minced
1 pound venison steak, cut into strips
2 tablespoons olive oil
1 large green pepper, cut into thin strips
1 red onion, thinly sliced
1 cup sliced fresh mushrooms
1/2 cup water
2 tablespoons cornstarch

Combine soy sauce, sugar and garlic. Add venison steak strips. Toss lightly and refrigerate for 3 - 4 hours. Drain steak. In a heavy skillet or wok, add olive oil and heat to medium high; add venison steak strips and stir fry for 3 - 4 minutes; add pepper, onion and mushrooms and stir fry for 3 - 4 additional minutes or until vegetables are tender crisp. Combine water and cornstarch and add to meat and vegetables, stirring constantly until thickened. Serve over rice, pasta or mashed potatoes.

STEAK AND POTATOES

1 pound venison cubed steak
2 tablespoons olive oil
1 (10¾-ounce) can cream of celery soup
1/2 cup milk
1/2 cup sour cream
1/4 teaspoon freshly ground black pepper
16 ounces frozen hash browns, thawed (cubed style)
1/2 cup shredded cheddar cheese, divided
1 (3-ounce) can french fried onions, divided

Brown venison steaks in olive oil in a skillet and set aside. Combine soup, milk, sour cream and pepper. Stir in thawed potatoes, 1/3 cup cheese, and 1/2 can onions. Spoon mixture into 9 x 13-inch baking dish. Arrange steaks over potatoes. Bake, covered, at 350°F for 45 - 50 minutes. Top with remaining cheese and onions and bake, uncovered, for 5 - 10 minutes longer.

THOUGHTS ON COOKING VENISON

Along with problems in cleaning and processing, improper cooking is the other prime culprit in turning off folks who eat venison. Quite simply, too much cooking can ruin many cuts of venison. The finest cuts—backstrap and tenderloin—should still be pink in the middle when taken from the grill, skillet or oven, and much the same is true of cubed steaks, ground venison and roasts. Indeed, the only time venison should be cooked for long periods of time is when it is used in soups, stews or similar dishes.

Using marinades, a meat hammer and good processing will make venison tender and tasty. Overcooking, on the other hand, will mean dry, relatively tasteless meat.

Loin Steaks with Onion Relish

LOIN STEAKS WITH ONION RELISH

 1 *pound venison loin steaks, cut ³/4-inch thick*
 ¼-1 *teaspoon coarsely ground black pepper*
 2 *tablespoons olive oil*
 1 *tablespoon butter or margarine*
 1 *tablespoon lemon juice*
 1 *large vidalia onion, thinly sliced and separated into rings*
 ½ *cup zinfandel wine*
 ½ *teaspoon dried basil, crushed*
 ¼ *teaspoon salt*

Rub both sides of steaks with ground pepper. In large non-stick skillet, heat olive oil and butter over medium-high heat; add steaks, drizzle with lemon juice and cook for about 4 minutes on each side for medium doneness. Remove the steaks and reserve drippings. Keep steaks warm.

Cook onion in drippings over medium heat for 5 - 7 minutes or until tender crisp. Add wine, basil and salt. Cook until most of the liquid has evaporated. Arrange steaks on plates and spoon onion relish on top.

SERVES 4

Tip: Leftovers make good sandwiches. Try them topped with mozzarella cheese. Broil to heat and melt cheese.

CRAB STUFFED VENISON STEAK ROLLS

STUFFING

¼-½	stick butter or margarine
1	garlic clove, minced
¼	cup chopped celery
¼	cup chopped onion
½	pound imitation crab, cut into small chunks (or the real thing)
1	tablespoon dried parsley
½	teaspoon dried cilantro
	Salt and pepper to taste

Melt butter; add garlic, celery and onion; sauté vegetables until soft. Add crab meat, herbs, salt and pepper. Remove from pan.

STEAKS AND WINE SAUCE

2	tablespoons butter or margarine
1	garlic clove, minced
4	venison cubed steaks (flatten if necessary)
4	large slices onion
1	cup zinfandel wine
½	cup sour cream
	Salt and pepper

Add butter to pan and lightly cook garlic; add steaks and quickly brown on both sides. Remove from pan and let cool enough to handle. Place stuffing in the center of steaks and roll. Secure with as many toothpicks as needed. Cut 4 large slices of onion and place in the pan. Place steak rolls on top of each onion slice. Pour wine over steaks. Cover and simmer for 15 - 20 minutes or until tender. Carefully remove onion and steak rolls from pan and place on a dish. Add sour cream to pan drippings and cook, stirring constantly until warm but not boiling. Salt and pepper to taste. Pour over steaks and serve immediately.

MUSTARD FRIED VENISON STEAKS

1	pound venison cubed steaks
½	cup prepared mustard
⅔	cup flour
1	teaspoon salt
6	tablespoons canola oil

Brush venison cubed steaks on both sides with prepared mustard. Mix flour and salt and dredge mustard-painted steaks in flour. Heat canola oil in a skillet and quickly cook floured steaks until golden brown. Serve immediately.

Tip: Any kind of mustard works well—try yellow, brown, Dijon or whatever you like best. An inexpensive paint brush makes "painting" the steaks quick and easy.

GREEK VENISON WRAP

3	slices bacon
1	small vidalia onion, thinly sliced
4-5	medium mushrooms, thinly sliced
½	teaspoon sugar
1	venison loin, thinly sliced
	Lemon pepper (to taste)
1	teaspoon lemon juice
2	tortilla wraps, warmed
2	tablespoons sour cream
	Fresh spinach leaves
3-4	tablespoons feta cheese, crumbled

Fry bacon in a skillet until brown; remove from pan, crumble and set aside. Add onion and mushrooms to pan and sauté until onions are translucent. Add sugar and stir well. Add venison and sprinkle generously with lemon pepper. Add lemon juice and sauté until venison is cooked (but still pink). Warm tortillas in microwave with a damp paper towel on top. Place sour cream in the center of tortilla, add several leaves of spinach, feta cheese, crumbled bacon and venison mixture. Wrap and serve immediately.

SERVES 2

HONEY AND MUSTARD STEAKS WITH ONION MUSHROOM WINE SAUCE

1 pound cubed venison steaks

HONEY AND MUSTARD SAUCE

¹/₃ cup stone-ground mustard with horseradish
*   (or your favorite Dijon-style mustard)*
1 teaspoon Italian seasonings
2 tablespoons honey
1 tablespoon cider vinegar
1 tablespoon water
2 tablespoons wine
¹/₈ teaspoon coarsely ground black pepper

Combine mustard sauce ingredients. Place cubed steaks in grilling pan (or non-stick fry pan) and brush both sides with sauce. Grill 8 - 10 minutes turning steaks and brushing with sauce. Meanwhile, prepare Onion Mushroom Wine Sauce.

ONION MUSHROOM WINE SAUCE

2 tablespoons olive oil
1 small onion, sliced
1 cup sliced mushrooms
2 tablespoons sugar
¹/₄ cup wine

Place olive oil in small fry pan and heat. Add onions, mushrooms and sugar and sauté briefly. Add wine and continue to cook until wine is reduced by half. Pour over Honey Mustard Cubed Steaks and serve immediately.

VENISON PHILLY SANDWICH

³/₄ pound venison loin, cut into thin strips
*   Italian salad dressing*
3 tablespoons butter or margarine
*   Several slices of sweet onion*
4-5 mushrooms
*   Bread and cheese of your choice*

Place sliced venison in bowl and cover with Italian dressing. Marinate for about 30 minutes. Melt butter in a small fry pan; sauté onion and mushrooms until tender. Drain venison and add to onion/mushroom mixture. Cook for about 2 minutes or until loin is still slightly pink. Meanwhile, place sliced bread and cheese under broiler to melt cheese. Top with loin mixture and serve immediately open-face style.

<u>SERVES 1</u>

CROCKPOT CUBED STEAK AND GRAVY

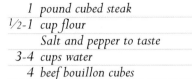

1	pound cubed steak
1/2-1	cup flour
	Salt and pepper to taste
3-4	cups water
4	beef bouillon cubes
1	tablespoon Worcestershire sauce

Coat steaks with flour, salt and pepper. Place steaks in crockpot. Add remaining flour mixture. Add 3 - 4 cups water, bouillon cubes and Worcestershire sauce. Cook on high setting for 45 minutes. Reduce setting to low and cook for 3 - 4 hours. Serve with mashed potatoes, green beans and applesauce for a comforting meal.

Tip: Remember that the bouillon cubes have salt and adjust your seasoning. Some cooks prefer to add more Worcestershire sauce (up to 4 tablespoons). If you don't lower the heat, all the gravy will cook away.

TERIYAKI VENISON

1 pound cubed venison steaks, cut into thin strips

MARINADE

1/2	cup soy sauce
2	tablespoons brown sugar
1	garlic clove, minced
1/4	teaspoon ground ginger

Mix soy sauce, brown sugar, garlic and ginger and add steak strips. Marinate for 30 - 45 minutes.

4	tablespoons butter or margarine
1	small onion, sliced
1	cup fresh mushrooms
1	cup bell pepper strips

Melt butter and sauté vegetables until tender. Push to side of pan and add venison steak strips which have been drained well. Sauté until steak is done; serve over rice.

CUTS FROM VENISON

The way you get your venison processed is largely a matter of personal choice. Some folks favor using everything possible for steaks or roasts; others prefer to have most of the carcass ground or cut into chunks for stew. Our suggestion is that you give some thought to your preferred dishes and have the meat processed accordingly.

For example, those who enjoy Tex-Mex or Italian dishes that make use of ground meat may want everything but the choicest of cuts done this way. A good general approach is to keep the backstraps and tenderloins whole (or butterflied), have the back hams prepared as roasts or cubed steak, and make ground or stew meat out of the remainder of the animal. You might try a roast out of the front shoulder, if it is not shot up.

BASIL VENISON

1 pound cubed venison steaks, cut into thin strips
Italian salad dressing

Slice and/or chop mixed fresh vegetables of your choice: onion, yellow squash, zucchini, carrots, sugar snap peas (if frozen, defrost). Place strips of steak in nonmetal container and cover with Italian salad dressing. Marinate for at least 30 minutes (3 - 4 hours is better).

BASIL BUTTER

  2 ounces fresh basil (2 bunches)
10 ounces butter or margarine
  1 large garlic clove, minced
1/8 teaspoon black pepper
  4 tablespoons grated Parmesan cheese

Remove large stems from basil and wash. Shake off excess water and dry. Place basil in a food processor. Add other ingredients and pulse until basil is chopped and all the ingredients are mixed well. Store in refrigerator and use as needed. Keeps for 7 days.

Cook vegetables in basil butter until partially done. Drain venison and add to vegetables. Continue cooking until venison is done. Serve immediately over rice.

Tip: Also try this basil butter with pasta and shrimp; it is delicious.

CHILI STEAK AND SALSA

      1 teaspoon chili powder
  1-2 garlic cloves, finely minced
    1/2 teaspoon salt
    1/2 teaspoon black pepper
  3/4-1 pound cubed venison steaks
      1 tablespoon olive oil
1/4-1/2 cup prepared salsa

Combine chili powder, garlic, salt and pepper. Rub evenly into both sides of steaks. Place olive oil in non-stick skillet over medium heat until hot. Add steaks and cook to desired doneness (for about 8 minutes). Turn steaks to brown evenly. Serve immediately with prepared salsa placed on top of each steak.

Tip: For a special treat, prepare a fresh tomato salsa.

BOURBON MUSTARD STEAK

  1 pound cubed venison steaks
     Salt and pepper to taste
  2 tablespoons Dijon mustard
  2 tablespoons butter or margarine
  2 tablespoons olive oil
  2 green onions, chopped
  2 tablespoons bourbon
  1 can mushrooms, drained
1/4 teaspoon dried chives
1/4 teaspoon dried parsley
1/4 teaspoon dried Italian seasoning
  4 tablespoons sour cream

Season steaks with salt and pepper and spread mustard generously on both sides of steaks. Melt butter in skillet and add olive oil. Brown steaks quickly on medium-high heat until desired doneness is reached. Do not overcook. Remove steaks. Add green onions and sauté. Add bourbon and cook until most of the liquid evaporates. Add mushrooms, herbs and sour cream, blending thoroughly with pan juices. Pour over steaks and serve immediately with rice.

CHIVE STEAKS

1 pound cubed venison steaks

CHIVE BUTTER

1/4 cup butter or margarine, at room temperature
2-3 tablespoons fresh chives, chopped
  2 teaspoons freshly squeezed lemon juice
1/2 teaspoon salt
1/4 teaspoon pepper

In a small bowl, combine butter, chives, lemon juice, salt and pepper. Using a fork, mix vigorously until blended. Place about half the butter mixture in a sauté pan over medium-high heat. Add steaks and cook quickly to desired doneness. Just before removing from pan, place a bit of the butter mixture on each steak and allow to melt before removing steaks. Serve immediately.

SERVES 4

Tip: Try broiled tomatoes with steaks.

Cubed Steak Italiano

CUBED STEAK ITALIANO

2 tablespoons olive oil
1 pound cubed venison steaks, cut into strips
1 onion, sliced
1 green pepper, cut into strips
1 garlic clove, minced
1 cup sliced mushrooms
1 (26-ounce) jar meatless spaghetti sauce
1 teaspoon dried basil
  Salt and pepper to taste

In a large skillet, heat olive oil and sauté steak strips, onion, green pepper, garlic and mushrooms until done. Stir in spaghetti sauce, basil, salt and pepper. Cover and simmer for 15 - 30 minutes to blend flavors. Serve over pasta of your choice.

<u>SERVES 4</u>

ITALIAN VENISON

1/4 cup flour
    Salt and pepper
1 pound cubed venison steaks
2 tablespoons canola oil
1 onion, sliced
2 garlic cloves, minced
1 (26-ounce) jar prepared spaghetti sauce
1 teaspoon oregano

Flour and season steaks. Brown steaks in hot canola oil in a skillet. Place in casserole dish. If needed, add more canola oil and sauté onions and garlic. Place on top of steaks. Pour spaghetti sauce over top and sprinkle with oregano. Cover and bake at 350°F for 1 hour or until tender. Serve with Caesar salad, garlic spaghetti and freshly grated Parmesan cheese.

PAPRIKA VENISON

1/3 cup butter or margarine
1 large onion, chopped
2 garlic cloves, minced
2 pounds boneless venison stew meat, cut into
    1/2-inch cubes
1 tablespoon paprika
1 teaspoon salt
    pepper
1/2 cup water
2 tablespoons flour
1 cup sour cream

Melt butter in Dutch oven. Add onion and garlic. Cook until tender but not brown. Remove from pan and set aside. Brown meat in remaining margarine over moderate heat. Add paprika to meat and margarine and stir about 1 minute. Return onion and garlic, and add salt, pepper and water. Cover and simmer for 1 1/2 - 2 hours. Add more water if necessary. Combine flour and sour cream, stir into meat mixture and cook until smooth and thickened. Do not boil. Serve with pasta.

Serves 6

UPGREN VENISON STROGANOFF

2 pounds venison steak, cut 1/2-inch thick
2 cups chopped mushrooms
1 cup finely chopped onion
1/4 cup butter or shortening
3 beef bouillon cubes
1 cup boiling water
2 tablespoons tomato paste
1 teaspoon dry mustard
1/2 teaspoon salt
2 tablespoons flour
1/2 cup water
1 cup sour cream

Cut steak into strips 2 1/4 inches long. In large skillet, sauté fresh mushrooms and onion in butter until golden brown; remove from the pan. Brown meat on all sides. Dissolve bouillon cubes in water; pour over meat. Add tomato paste, mustard and salt. Heat to boiling, reduce heat, and simmer for 45 minutes or until tender. Combine flour and water. Slowly stir into meat mixture. Cook, stirring constantly, until mixture comes to a boil; reduce heat. Add mushrooms, onions and sour cream. Heat through but do not boil. Serve over hot rice or chow mein noodles.

Serves 4 - 6

STUFFED VENISON

1 boned rump roast, or rolled roast
1 cup Italian salad dressing
1 pound bulk pork sausage
    Salt and pepper to taste

Cover roast in Italian dressing and marinate in refrigerator for 4 - 8 hours. Drain and place pork sausage inside roast and roll. Tie or secure with toothpicks. Wrap in foil, place in roasting pan and bake at 400°F for 40-50 minutes or until done. (Use your meat thermometer to check on doneness).

Tip: A tenderloin is nice prepared in this manner. Try serving one loin stuffed with shrimp and one with sausage. One loin takes only about 1/2 pound sausage.

CREAMED VENISON

1 (10¾-ounce) can cream of mushroom soup
1 (10¾-ounce) can cream of celery soup
1 (10¾-ounce) can cream of potato soup
1 package dry onion soup mix
1 can water
2 pounds venison, cut into 2-inch chunks

Place all soups and water in a Dutch oven; mix well. Stir in venison chunks. Heat to boiling. Reduce heat, cover and simmer for 1 - 2 hours, until tender. Serve over rice.

SERVES 6 - 8

HASH BROWN POTATOES WITH VENISON

½ stick butter or margarine
1 small onion, diced
1 garlic clove, minced
1 pound cooked venison, diced very small
4 medium potatoes, cooked and diced
  Salt and pepper to taste
  Tabasco (a few dashes)

Melt butter in a large skillet; add onion and garlic and cook until tender. Add venison and potatoes. Season to taste. Mix and fry until browned. (Sometimes you may need to add more butter.) Serve when browned. Top with ketchup; serve along with eggs and toast for a hearty breakfast.

VENISON CROQUETTES

2 slices bacon, chopped and cooked
¼ cup finely chopped onion
1½-2 cups finely chopped cooked venison
½ cup cooked, crumbled, pork sausage
1 tablespoon currant jelly
1 teaspoon dry mustard
1 egg, slightly beaten
  Salt and pepper to taste

COATING

2 eggs, beaten
  Flour
  Fine bread crumbs
2-4 tablespoons canola oil

Sauté bacon and onion. Add to venison and sausage. Add jelly, mustard, egg, salt and pepper. Mix well and shape into 12 oval croquettes. Coat each croquette by dipping into beaten eggs, then flour and egg again; roll in bread crumbs.

Heat canola oil in fry pan and cook croquettes until golden brown.

SERVES 6

Crockpot Roast with Cranberries

CROCKPOT ROAST WITH CRANBERRIES

1	(10½-ounce) can double-strength beef broth
½	can water
¼	teaspoon ground cinnamon
2-3	teaspoons cream-style prepared horseradish
1	(16-ounce) can whole berry cranberry sauce
1	venison roast (3-4 pounds)
	Salt and pepper to taste

Place broth, water, cinnamon, horseradish and cranberry sauce in medium saucepan; heat to boiling while stirring constantly. Place venison roast in crockpot. Pour sauce over roast and cook on low for 6 - 8 hours or until roast is tender. Pass juice with roast.

SERVES 8

Tip: Leftovers are good cold, sliced for sandwiches.

JERKY

1½ pounds venison, partially frozen

MARINADE

¼	cup Worcestershire sauce
¼	cup soy sauce
1	teaspoon liquid smoke
1	teaspoon onion powder
½	teaspoon garlic powder
¼	teaspoon black pepper
	Several dashes hot sauce (Tabasco)

Partially freeze venison and slice into ¼-inch pieces. Mix marinade ingredients and add venison slices; marinate for 16 - 24 hours in refrigerator. Cover bottom rack of oven with foil. Place strips of venison on top rack. Set oven temperature on 150°F and crack door slightly. By cracking the door, temperature will be between 130 and 140°F (at 150°F the jerky tends to be too crunchy). Dry jerky for 6 - 8 hours. Store in airtight containers.

Tip: Partially freezing the venison makes slicing thinly much easier.

PARTY PÂTÉ

2	pounds venison, cooked
1	medium onion, chopped
1	garlic clove, minced
1	hard-cooked egg
½	cup Hellman's mayonnaise
1	stick butter, softened (do not substitute)
¼	cup bourbon (high quality)
½	teaspoon salt, or to taste
¼	teaspoon pepper, freshly ground, or to taste
	Bayleaf

Place venison, onion, garlic and egg in food processor and pulse until smooth. Add mayonnaise and softened butter and mix only enough to thoroughly blend. Add bourbon, salt and pepper and blend well. Mold into a ball and top with a bay leaf. Wrap securely with plastic wrap and refrigerate overnight. Remove bay leaf, garnish with chives and serve with Melba toast, party rye, or assorted crackers.

HAMBURGER STEAK WITH ONION TOPPING

2	tablespoons canola oil
1-1½	cups sliced sweet onions
1-2	tablespoons water
¼	teaspoon paprika
	Black pepper to taste
1	pound ground venison
	Salt to taste

Heat canola oil in large skillet and sauté onions until tender. Add water while sautéing onions if needed to prevent sticking. Stir paprika and black pepper into onions; remove onions from pan and keep warm. Season ground venison with salt and shape into 2 large 1-inch-thick patties. Put hamburger steaks in onion-flavored oil and cook over medium heat until browned on both sides and desired doneness is reached. Arrange steaks on 2 plates and top with reserved, cooked onions.

QUICK VENISON MAC

1/2 pound ground venison
1 small leek (or onion), chopped
1 garlic clove, minced
1 tablespoon olive oil
1 (14-ounce) can diced tomatoes
1 (8-ounce) can tomato sauce
1 cup water
1/4 teaspoon chili powder
1/8 teaspoon cumin
1/4 teaspoon sugar
1/4 teaspoon black pepper
1 cup uncooked elbow macaroni
3 tablespoons fresh oregano, chopped

In a skillet, brown venison, chopped leek and garlic in olive oil. Be sure to crumble venison as it cooks. Add tomatoes, tomato sauce and water and bring to a boil. Add all other ingredients except fresh oregano and return to a boil. Reduce heat, cover and simmer for 15 minutes or until macaroni is tender. Add oregano and serve immediately.

CHOPPED STEAK AND GRAVY

2 teaspoons dry beef onion soup mix
1 pound ground venison
1 teaspoon Worcestershire sauce
Salt and pepper to taste
2 tablespoons olive oil
2 tablespoons flour

Microwave onion soup mix in 1/4 cup water until onions are tender and add to ground venison with Worcestershire sauce, salt and pepper. Handle gently and form into patties. Place olive oil in a non-stick pan. Add patties and cook until done (6 - 8 minutes). Remove from pan. Add flour and make a roux. Stir constantly for 1 minute. Add 1 cup water (or more if needed) and stir until smooth and thick. Add patties and simmer for 10 - 15 minutes. Serve with rice.

VENISON EGGPLANT PARMIGIANA

1 large eggplant, or 3-4 small eggplants
Salt to taste
1 pound ground venison
1/2 cup chopped onion
2 garlic cloves, minced
1 tablespoon olive oil
1 (16-ounce) can diced tomatoes
1 (8-ounce) can tomato sauce
3 tablespoons fresh basil, chopped
1/2 teaspoon black pepper
1 tablespoon cherry preserves
1 egg, beaten
1/2 cup cracker crumbs (saltines)
1-2 tablespoons olive oil
2 cups shredded mozzarella cheese

Peel and slice eggplant, place on paper towels and sprinkle with salt; cover with more paper towels. Let set while preparing sauce.

In large skillet sauté venison, onion and garlic in 1 tablespoon of the olive oil until meat is no longer red. Add tomatoes, tomato sauce, basil, salt and pepper and cherry preserves. Stir well and simmer for 15 - 20 minutes.

Rinse eggplant and pat dry. Dip in egg and then cracker crumbs and quickly brown in remaining 1 - 2 tablespoons of the olive oil. Spray baking dish. Layer eggplant, 1 cup of the cheese, sauce and remaining 1 cup of the cheese. Bake at 350°F uncovered for 15 - 20 minutes or until bubbly and hot.

Deep Dish Potato and Venison Pie

DEEP DISH POTATO AND VENISON PIE

Pastry for double-crust pie (homemade or
   purchased)
1 cup grated, peeled potatoes
¹/4 cup chopped celery
¹/2 cup grated carrots
¹/4 cup chopped leeks
2 teaspoons Worcestershire sauce
1 teaspoon A-1 Steak Sauce
1 teaspoon dried Italian seasoning
¹/4 teaspoon freshly ground black pepper
   Salt to taste
1 pound uncooked ground venison

Place bottom crust in 9-inch deep dish pie
plate. Mix all other ingredients and place in pie
crust. Place top crust on pie and seal edges.
Cut vents in top pastry. Bake at 375°F for 15
minutes. Reduce heat to 350°F degrees and
bake for 55 - 60 minutes. This pie is hearty;
however, it is dry and needs to be served with
a sauce. We like this mushroom sauce.

MUSHROOM SAUCE

2 tablespoons butter or margarine
¹/4 cup sliced leeks
2 cups sliced fresh mushrooms (wild or button)
2 tablespoons flour
1 cup half-and-half
   Salt and pepper to taste

Melt butter and sauté leeks and mushrooms
until tender. Sprinkle with flour and cook for
about 1 minute. Add half-and-half and seasonings. Continue cooking until sauce has thickened. Stir constantly. Serve over pie slices.

*Tip: This sauce can also be used over steaks, chops or
wild rice with upland game.*

MEATBALLS IN CURRANT SAUCE

1½ pounds ground venison
½ cup dry bread crumbs
½ cup milk
1 egg, beaten
¼ cup finely minced onion
1½ teaspoons salt
¼ teaspoon pepper
¼ teaspoon garlic powder

Mix ingredients well and shape into 1-inch balls. Place in baking dish and brown in 350°F oven for 30 minutes. Drain well if needed.

Heat a 10-ounce jar red currant jelly and a 12-ounce jar chili sauce in a large skillet. Add meatballs and simmer for 30 minutes. Serve hot in a chafing dish.

CRANBERRY TOPPED MEAT LOAF

¼ cup cranberry sauce
⅛-¼ cup brown sugar
1 pound ground venison
½ cup quick cooking oats
½ cup milk
¼ cup finely chopped onion
⅛ cup ketchup
⅛ cup cocktail sauce
1 egg, lightly beaten
½ teaspoon Italian seasoning
⅛ teaspoon black pepper
½ teaspoon salt or to taste

Preheat oven to 350°F. Spray 9 x 5 x 3-inch loaf pan. In a small bowl, combine the cranberry sauce and brown sugar. Place sauce mixture in bottom of a loaf pan. In a large bowl, combine the remaining ingredients and mix well. Place in loaf pan on top of cranberry sauce mixture. Bake at 350°F for 1 hour. Allow loaf to cool for about 10 minutes before carefully turning onto a serving plate so that the sauce side is up. Serve immediately.

ENCHILADAS

12 corn tortillas
1-1½ pounds ground venison
1 medium onion, diced
3 cups Monterey Jack cheese

ENCHILADA SAUCE

1 (10¾-ounce) can cream of chicken soup
1 (10-ounce) can diced tomatoes and chiles
½ cup diced onion
1 (4-ounce) can chopped green chiles

Wrap tortillas in foil and place in moderate oven to soften (8 - 10 minutes). Meanwhile, sauté ground venison and onion in skillet until venison is done and onion is tender. Place a little meat and onion mixture on each softened tortilla, add a little cheese, roll up tortilla and place in lightly greased baking dish.

Mix all sauce ingredients together and pour over rolled tortillas. Pour any remaining meat over sauce. Top with remaining cheese. Bake in a 350°F oven until hot and bubbly (about 20 - 30 minutes).

SERVES 6

BACON MUSHROOM SWISS MEAT LOAF

4 slices bacon, diced
1 cup chopped mushrooms
¼ cup finely chopped onion
1 pound ground venison
1 egg
¼ cup milk
1 cup shredded Swiss cheese
½ cup very fine Corn Flakes crumbs
¼ teaspoon salt
⅛ teaspoon black pepper

In large skillet, cook bacon until crisp. Remove bacon with slotted spoon and drain on paper towels. Remove all but one tablespoon of bacon drippings; sauté the mushrooms and onions in drippings until tender. Allow to cool slightly. In a large bowl, mix the venison, egg and milk. Add the mushroom/onion mixture, Swiss cheese (except for a few tablespoons), bacon crumbs (except for a tablespoon), Corn Flakes crumbs; salt and pepper; mix well until blended. Place in a large loaf pan and bake at 350°F for 1 hour or until cooked through. If your ground venison is not lean, drain the fat. Sprinkle top of meatloaf with reserved cheese and bacon. Bake for an additional 5 minutes or until cheese melts. Let meatloaf rest for 10 minutes before slicing.

<u>SERVES</u> 4 - 6

E. T.'S MEAT LOAF

1½-2 pounds ground venison
1 package dry onion soup mix
1 cup oats, regular or quick cooking (not instant)
1 egg, slightly beaten
½ cup applesauce
½ cup ketchup, divided
Black pepper (to taste)

Thoroughly mix all ingredients using only ¼ cup of the ketchup. Place in loaf pan and bake at 350°F for 45 - 50 minutes. Remove from oven and top with remaining ¼ cup of the ketchup. Return to oven for 10 - 15 minutes or until top is browned and meat loaf is done.

Tip: The applesauce really makes this meat loaf moist and tasty.

USE OF ORGAN MEATS

Organ meats from venison, including the heart, liver and kidneys, can be quite tasty, and they are better for you than the same organs from beef.

Unlike the remainder of the deer, organ meats do not require aging. They should be separated when the animal is field dressed, and many hunters carry a heavy-duty, sealable plastic bag in which to store them once the animal has been gutted.

Working up organs is easily done at home, and many processors are reluctant to handle them. Slice or otherwise prepare the organ meat with an eye to your plans for its future use. Slicing or dicing is most common, and even though you may eventually mince or blend the meat when used in pâté, this is best done after cooking. There are many delicious dishes which can be prepared from the organs, a consideration worth keeping in mind once you have your animal on the ground.

ITALIAN BURGERS

1 egg
1/4 cup oats, regular or quick cooking (do not use instant)
2 tablespoons ketchup
3/4 teaspoon dried Italian seasoning
1 garlic clove, finely minced
2 tablespoons finely chopped onion
1/4 teaspoon salt
1 pound ground venison
4 mozzarella cheese slices
4 hamburger buns or rolls

Lightly beat egg with a fork and stir in oats. Add ketchup, Italian seasoning, garlic, onion, salt and ground venison. Mix well and shape into 4 patties. Broil or grill patties about 12 minutes or until desired doneness is reached, turning once. Top with cheese and broil until cheese melts. Serve on toasted buns with ketchup, lettuce and tomatoes.

FETA BURGERS

1 cup plain yogurt
1/4 cup feta cheese
1/4-1/2 teaspoon ground cumin
1 pound ground venison
1/4 cup finely diced onion
1/2 teaspoon dried cilantro, or to taste
Several dashes of ground ginger, or to taste
Salt to taste
Lettuce
Cucumbers, thinly sliced
Pita bread

Blend yogurt, feta cheese and cumin with a fork until the cheese is finely crumbled. Cover and refrigerate for 1 hour. Combine ground venison, onion, cilantro, ginger and salt to taste. Shape into 4 patties and grill, broil or pan fry until done. Place lettuce and cucumbers in pita bread, add burger and top with 2 tablespoons yogurt sauce.

SERVES 4

BLUE CHEESE BURGERS

1 pound ground venison
1/4 cup finely chopped onion
1/4 cup crumbled blue cheese
1 teaspoon Worcestershire sauce
1/4 teaspoon salt
1/8 teaspoon freshly ground black pepper

Mix all ingredients thoroughly but gently and shape into 4 patties. Grill over hot coals (for about 4 minutes per side) or until burgers have reached desired doneness. Serve on grilled hamburger buns with lots of crisp lettuce, tomato slices and mayonnaise.

SERVES 4

Tip: These can be broiled or cooked in a grilling pan. If grilling, oil the grill top to prevent sticking.

BURGERS WITH BUILT-IN CONDIMENTS

1 pound ground venison
2 tablespoons ketchup
1 tablespoon A-1 Steak Sauce
2 teaspoons mustard
1/2 teaspoon Worcestershire sauce
Several dashes freshly ground black pepper

Thoroughly mix all condiments into ground venison. Form into patties, being careful to form well because condiments make burgers softer. Grill to desired doneness and serve on onion rolls with lettuce, tomato, onion and pickles.

Mexican Burgers

MEXICAN BURGERS

  1 pound ground venison
  ¼ cup finely chopped onion
½-1 teaspoon chili powder (or to taste)
  ¼ teaspoon ground cumin
  ½ teaspoon finely minced jalapeño pepper
        (or to taste)
  ½ teaspoon salt
  ¼ teaspoon black pepper

Combine all ingredients well and shape into 4 patties. Grill, broil or pan fry to desired doneness. Serve burgers on tortillas (cut burgers in half for a better fit), pita bread, English muffins or hamburger buns with traditional taco toppings of your choice. The toppings might include salsa, shredded cheese, guacamole or chopped avocado, sour cream, lettuce and diced green onions. Serve with Corona and lime wedges or Mexican beer.

Venison

COOKOUT TIME BURGERS

2 pounds ground venison

Handle ground venison gently and form into 8 patties. Grill to desired doneness (for about 4 - 5 minutes per side) and serve with a variety of buns and Mustard Sauce, Herb Mayonnaise, Horseradish Spread, Bacon Bean Topping, and Double Red Topping. Sit back and listen to the raves.

SERVES 6 - 8

MUSTARD SAUCE

½ cup mayonnaise
¾ cup sour cream
1 teaspoon dry mustard
2 teaspoons spicy brown mustard

Using a wire whisk, mix above ingredients well. Serve as a condiment for venison burgers.

SERVES 6 - 8

HERB MAYONNAISE

3 tablespoons mayonnaise
1 teaspoon Dijon mustard
1 teaspoon dried basil leaves
¼ teaspoon parsley
½ teaspoon garlic salt
¼ teaspoon freshly ground black pepper

Mix above ingredients well using a wire whisk. Serve as a venison burger condiment.

SERVES 4

HORSERADISH SPREAD

½ cup plain yogurt (or sour cream)
1 tablespoon prepared horseradish
1 teaspoon Dijon mustard

Blend ingredients well and use as a spread for venison burgers instead of mustard or mayonnaise.

SERVES 4

BACON BEAN TOPPING

4 slices bacon
¼-½ cup chopped onion
1 (16-ounce) can baked beans
2 tablespoons mustard

Pan fry bacon slices until crisp. Drain on paper towels and then crumble. Add onion to bacon drippings and sauté until tender. Add beans and mustard to onions and heat thoroughly. Place in bowl and top with crumbled bacon. Serve over venison burgers or hot dogs.

SERVES 4 - 6

DOUBLE RED TOPPING

2 tablespoons olive oil
2 teaspoons lemon juice
1 teaspoon dried basil (or 1 tablespoon fresh basil)
Salt and freshly ground black pepper
Sliced ripe tomatoes
Sliced red onions

Mix olive oil and lemon juice with a wire whisk until well blended. Add basil and seasonings; pour over sliced ripe tomatoes and sliced red onions. Serve over venison burgers or as a side dish.

SERVES 4

Tip: Brush grill top with oil to prevent burgers from sticking. Avoid frequent flipping of burgers.

MUSTARD BURGERS

1 teaspoon Worcestershire sauce
1 pound ground venison
   Mustard (such as Spicy Brown Mustard)

Mix Worcestershire sauce into ground venison
and form into patties. Brush mustard onto both
sides of patties and grill (using a grilling pan). Do
not have heat too high or mustard will burn. Turn
frequently and continue to lightly coat with mustard. Burgers are best if still slightly pink on the
inside. Serve with lettuce, tomatoes, pickles and
mustard on whole wheat buns.

CHILI SAUCE FOR BURGERS
OR HOT DOGS

2 tablespoons canola oil
1/2 cup finely chopped onion
2 garlic cloves, minced
1 pound ground venison, finely ground
1/2 teaspoon salt
1/2 teaspoon freshly ground black pepper
1 tablespoon yellow mustard
1 tablespoon cider vinegar
1 teaspoon Worcestershire sauce
   Several dashes hot sauce, to taste
1/4 cup ketchup
1 cup tomato juice

Heat canola oil to medium heat in a large heavy
skillet and sauté onion and garlic until tender. Do
not brown. Add venison and cook until meat is
browned; stir frequently to break up any chunks
of meat. Add remaining ingredients, bring to a
boil, reduce heat and simmer until sauce has
thickened. You may need more or less tomato
juice to maintain the correct consistency. Serve
over venison burgers with mustard, slaw and
onions for a delicious treat or as a topping for hot
dogs.

<u>SERVES 6 - 8</u>

*Tip: The secret to chili sauce is a uniform, non-chunky
consistency. Try grinding the venison yourself in your
food processor or blender. It needs to be very fine.*

Venison

Venison and Your Health

There are a number of health-related issues, most of them of a positive nature, which should be kept in mind when eating venison.

The lean, red meat is quite low in fat, and for that matter, any fat which is present should be trimmed off during processing. The same is true of sinew and membranes. Indeed, an expert writing in *The Nutrition Letter* of January, 1990, noted that it is important "to understand that cholesterol is an integral part of the cell membrane of animals and so the cholesterol content of meat is more closely tied to the membranes of muscle cells than to the fat content of the muscle." By removing both fat and "white" membrane from venison, you reduce what is already a relatively low level of cholesterol content. That is why venison is the only red meat some heart patients are allowed to eat.

Other pluses include the fact that no venison from the wild has ever been exposed to inoculants, questionable food supplements, hormones or other artificial additions to the animal's diet.

One word of caution does need to be sounded in connection with venison, and it is not as widely known as it should be. Any woman who is pregnant or thinks she might be pregnant should avoid all contact with raw or rare venison, and to be truly safe, she probably should not eat venison at all. Exposure can result in the disease known as toxoplasmosis. A woman who becomes infected risks major problems with the fetus she is carrying. These include but are not limited to brain damage, hydrocephaly, jaundice, convulsions at or shortly after birth, and even death. If pregnant women do eat venison, it should be cooked until all pinkness is gone and at levels above 165°F.

ZITI

	1	pound ground venison
1/4-1/2		pound bulk venison sausage
	1/2	cup chopped onions
	2	garlic cloves, minced
	3 1/2	cups meatless spaghetti sauce
	1	cup chicken broth
	1	tablespoon chopped fresh oregano
	1	tablespoon chopped fresh parsley
	16	ounces ziti, cooked and drained
	2	cups shredded mozzarella cheese, divided
	1	cup grated Parmesan cheese, divided

In a large skillet over medium-high heat, sauté ground venison, sausage, onions and garlic for 6 - 8 minutes until venison is browned. Stir in spaghetti sauce, chicken broth, oregano and parsley. Reduce heat; simmer for 10 - 15 minutes. Stir 1 cup of the sauce into ziti. Spoon half the ziti mixture into 9 x 13-inch baking dish. Sprinkle with 1 1/2 cups of the mozzarella and 1/2 cup of the Parmesan cheese. Top with 2 cups of the sauce, then remaining ziti mixture and sauce. Cover and bake at 350°F for 20 minutes. Sprinkle with remaining 1/2 cup of the mozzarella and remaining 1/2 cup of the Parmesan cheese. Bake uncovered for 10 minutes longer or until heated through, cheese has melted, and ziti is bubbly.

SERVES 8

Tip: Try adding a cup of ricotta cheese in the center with the mozzarella and Parmesan.

SPEEDY MEAT SAUCE

1 1/2	pounds ground venison
2	tablespoons olive oil
1/2	cup onion
2	garlic cloves, minced
1	(14-ounce) can stewed tomatoes, cut up
1	(6-ounce) can V-8 or tomato juice
1	(14-ounce) jar meatless spaghetti sauce
1	teaspoon grape jelly
1/2	teaspoon oregano
1/2	teaspoon basil

Brown meat in olive oil along with onion and garlic. Stir in other ingredients. Cook for 15 - 20 minutes or until jelly melts. Serve over pasta.

SIMPLE SPAGHETTI SAUCE

3	tablespoons olive oil
1	medium onion, chopped
4	garlic cloves, minced
1	pound fresh mushrooms, sliced
1	pound bulk venison sausage
1	pound ground venison
2	(16-ounce) cans diced tomatoes
2	(6-ounce) cans tomato paste
2	tablespoons minced parsley
1 1/2	teaspoons oregano
1	teaspoon salt
1	teaspoon pepper
1	cup merlot or other red wine

Heat olive oil in Dutch oven and sauté onion, garlic and mushrooms. In skillet, brown sausage and ground venison; add to Dutch oven. Add remaining ingredients; cover and simmer for about 2 hours or until sauce has thickened and flavors have blended. Serve over pasta.

SERVES 6 - 8

Tip: If you like a hot and spicy sauce, try adding 1 - 2 tablespoons canned jalapeño peppers (along with some of the juice) to the sauce.

SPAGHETTI AND MEATBALLS

SAUCE

- 3/4 cup chopped onion
- 2 garlic cloves, minced
- 1 tablespoon olive oil
- 1 1/2 cups water
- 1 (16-ounce) can tomato sauce
- 1 (12-ounce) can tomato paste
- 1/4 cup minced fresh parsley
- 1/2 tablespoon dried basil
- 1/2 tablespoon dried oregano
- 1 teaspoon salt
- 1/4 teaspoon black pepper

In Dutch oven over medium heat, sauté onion and garlic in olive oil. Add water, tomato sauce and tomato paste, parsley, basil, oregano, salt and pepper; heat to boiling. Reduce heat; cover and simmer for about 1 hour.

MEATBALLS

- 1 1/2 pounds ground venison
- 2 eggs, lightly beaten
- 1 cup soft bread crumbs (use a blender to make fine crumbs)
- 3/4 cup milk
- 1/2 cup grated Parmesan cheese
- 2 garlic cloves, minced
- 1 teaspoon salt
- 1/2 teaspoon black pepper

Combine meatball ingredients and mix well. Shape into 1 1/2-inch balls. Place meatballs on a cookie sheet and refrigerate for several hours (or in freezer for 15 - 20 minutes). Place 2 tablespoons olive oil in large skillet over medium heat and add meatballs. Brown meatballs on all sides and add to sauce. Simmer for about 30 minutes, stirring occasionally. Stir very gently to avoid tearing up meatballs. Serve over spaghetti.

SERVES 6

Tip: Chilling is the secret to keeping meatballs whole.

HERBED MEAT SAUCE

- 1 tablespoon olive oil
- 1 medium onion, chopped
- 2-3 garlic cloves, minced
- 1 pound ground venison
- 1/2 pound Italian sausage, removed from casings
- 1 (14-ounce) can whole tomatoes
- 1 (14-ounce) can diced tomatoes
- 1 (8-ounce) can tomato sauce
- 3/4 cup water
- 1 teaspoon sugar
- 1/2 teaspoon salt
- 1/2 cup fresh basil and oregano, chopped and packed
- 1/8 teaspoon black pepper
- 1 pound spaghetti, cooked

Heat olive oil in a large, deep skillet over medium heat. Add onion and garlic and cook until onions are translucent. Add venison and sausage and cook until meat is no longer pink. Add remaining sauce ingredients and heat to boiling. Reduce heat and simmer (covered) for 1 hour or until sauce thickens slightly. Add sauce to drained pasta and top with freshly grated Parmesan cheese.

SERVES 6

Tip: This is a low-cost meal. The sauce freezes well.

COOKOUT SALAD

- 1 pound ground venison
- 1 package taco seasoning mix
- 1/2 cup water
- 1 head lettuce, shredded
- 1 green pepper, chopped
- 1 onion, chopped
- 2 tomatoes, chopped
- 1 (16-ounce) can red kidney beans, rinsed, drained
- 1-2 cups grated cheddar cheese
- 12-16 ounces tortilla chips, crushed
- 1 (8-ounce) bottle Catalina salad dressing

Brown ground venison in a skillet. Add taco seasoning and water; simmer until thickened and flavors are blended. Cool slightly. Place remaining ingredients (except dressing) in a large salad bowl, add cooked venison, top with dressing and toss to mix well. Serve immediately.

SAUSAGE MEATBALL SUBS

MEATBALLS

1/2	pound ground venison
1/2	pound bulk venison sausage
1/2	cup Parmesan cheese
1/4	cup milk
1	cup soft bread crumbs
1/4	cup finely chopped onions
1	egg, beaten
1/2	teaspoon garlic salt
1/4	teaspoon black pepper
1/4	teaspoon basil
1/4	teaspoon oregano
1	tablespoon parsley
1/4	teaspoon lemon juice

Lightly mix all meatball ingredients. Be gentle and handle the meatballs as little as possible for best results. Shape into 1-inch meatballs and place on a cookie sheet. Place in freezer to get meatballs very cold before cooking (for about 10 minutes).

SAUCE

2	tablespoons olive oil
1/2	large red onion
1/2	cup sliced fresh mushrooms
1/2	large green bell pepper, cut into thin strips (optional)
1/4	teaspoon sugar
1	(14-ounce) jar prepared meatless spaghetti sauce
4	hoagie rolls
1	cup shredded mozzarella cheese

In a large non-stick skillet, heat olive oil and add onion, mushrooms and peppers. Sauté until the vegetables are tender. Sprinkle sugar over veggies, stir well and remove from the pan. Add meatballs (which have been chilled thoroughly) to pan and sauté until brown and no longer pink in the center (about 15 minutes). Turn meatballs gently to keep from breaking up. Add spaghetti sauce and vegetables to meatballs and simmer for 5 - 8 minutes until all ingredients are hot.

Split hoagie rolls, place on a baking sheet, and sprinkle with mozzarella cheese. Bake at 400°F until cheese melts (about 5 minutes). Spoon meatballs and sauce over rolls. Serve immediately.

SERVES 4

Tip: To make soft bread crumbs, place torn bread slices in blender container and pulse on and off until bread is fine crumbs. Two slices of bread make about 1 cup of soft bread crumbs.

VENISON SAUSAGE BAKED BEANS

½-1 pound bulk venison sausage
  1 onion, chopped
  4 cups undrained, canned, pork and beans
  1 cup drained, canned, lima beans
  1 cup drained, canned, kidney beans
½ cup brown sugar (or pancake syrup)
  1 cup ketchup
  2 tablespoons mustard
  2 teaspoons Worcestershire sauce
½ teaspoon chili powder (optional)
  4 slices bacon

Crumble sausage and cook until no longer pink. Add onion before sausage is completely done and cook until onion is tender crisp. If you have any fat, drain well. Add all other ingredients except bacon and mix well. Place in a 9 x 13-inch pan, top with bacon slices, and bake at 350°F for about 1 hour or until beans are as thick as you desire.

Tip: This is good for cookouts, buffets or covered dish dinners. This can also be cooked in the crockpot on low for about 4 hours. For variation, ground venison can be substituted for the sausage.

SCOTCH EGGS

  1 pound bulk venison sausage
½-1 teaspoon dried sage (or to taste)
¼ teaspoon cayenne pepper
  4 large eggs, hard boiled, peeled
½ cup flour
  2 eggs, lightly beaten
  1 cup fresh bread crumbs
  Vegetable oil for frying

Combine sausage, sage and cayenne pepper. Mix well and divide into 4 equal portions; flatten each portion into a thin round on wax paper. Enclose each hard-boiled egg completely in a sausage round. Pat sausage into place to cover egg completely. Dredge sausage-coated eggs in flour, dip in beaten eggs, and roll gently in bread crumbs to coat well. Heat vegetable oil to 350°F and deep fry Scotch eggs for about 10 minutes or until done. Remove with slotted spoon and drain well on paper towels.

S<small>ERVES</small> 4

Tip: These are nice for a snack while afield, for a picnic, or sliced for an appetizer.

SAUSAGE GRAVY

  2 tablespoons butter or margarine
¾-1 cup cooked, crumbled, venison sausage
    (½-¾ pound uncooked)
  2 tablespoons flour
  1 cup milk
  1 teaspoon Worcestershire sauce
  Salt and pepper to taste

Melt butter in a fry pan. Add cooked sausage and stir to break up and heat through. Add flour and cook about 1 minute. Add milk and Worcestershire sauce. Season to taste. Cook until thickened and serve over toast or hot biscuits.

S<small>ERVES</small> 2

Tip: This is a good way to use leftover sausage; however, if no leftovers are available you can just cook your sausage and then add the margarine and flour and continue as above.

RED BEANS AND RICE

1 cup regular, long-grain rice
2 tablespoons olive oil
1 cup chopped celery
2 garlic cloves, minced
1 cup chopped sweet onion
½ teaspoon dried thyme
½ teaspoon dried oregano
½ teaspoon dried parsley
1 bay leaf
1 (15-ounce) can, red kidney beans, rinsed and drained
¼ cup chopped ham
1 cup cooked bulk venison sausage, crumbled
    and drained
1 cup low-salt chicken broth
½ teaspoon Worcestershire sauce
    Salt and pepper to taste
    Hot pepper sauce to taste

Prepare rice as directed on label and keep warm. Meanwhile, in 3-quart pan, heat olive oil and add celery, garlic and onion. Cook until tender crisp; add herbs, rinsed and drained beans, ham, cooked sausage, chicken broth and Worcestershire sauce. Simmer for 10 - 15 minutes. Season to taste and serve over hot rice.

Tip: The flavor of the herbs decreases the need for salt for those on low-sodium diets.

MENUS FOR VENISON

Spicy Tomato Juice Cocktail

Loin Steaks with Crab, Shrimp and
Scallop Sauce*

Garlic Spaghetti

Wild Strawberry Spinach Salad*

Hot Crunchy Rolls

Ice Cream Pie with
Black Walnut Crust*

White Zinfandel Wine or Hazelnut
Cream Coffee

✦ ✦ ✦ ✦ ✦ ✦ ✦ ✦ ✦

Meatballs in Currant Sauce*

Cook Out Time Burgers*

Hot Dogs

Chili Sauce for Burgers or
Hot Dogs*

Onion Rolls and Buns

Venison Sausage Baked Beans*

Cole Slaw

Etah's Artichoke Relish*

Assorted Pickles and Chips

Wild Strawberry Trifle*

Lemonade or Iced Beer

*Recipe included in cookbook

WILD TURKEY

The American wild turkey holds a proud and prominent place in our nation's culinary history. At an early age, schoolchildren learn of the manner in which wild turkeys graced the Pilgrims' tables at the first Thanksgiving celebration, and stories of how America's big game bird offered fine fare on frontier tables fill fictional and factual chronicles of pioneer life. Wild turkeys were incredibly abundant during the early years of European settlement, and surprisingly, given the quarry's modern-day wariness, hunters experienced little trouble in killing them for personal use and the market.

In time, an increasing human presence, roost shooting, the absence of hunting seasons or a conservation ethic, and general prodigality, changed all this. Turkeys disappeared from much of their original range, and by the dawn of the 20th century they had become so scarce as to be a gourmet delight denied all but a select few.

But even then, those privileged to live in regions where there were still wild turkeys—and possessed of sufficient savvy and skill to hunt them successfully—recognized the bird's grand

attributes when it came to fine dining. For example, the enduring stories of a grand old Southern sporting scribe, Archibald Rutledge, are laced with descriptions of holiday feasts featuring a wild turkey as the centerpiece. Similar circumstances existed in the home of another South Carolinian, Henry Edwards Davis, author of *The American Wild Turkey* (which many authorities consider the single finest book ever written on turkey hunting). Davis' daughter, Virginia Carroll, tenders a delightful anecdote of her youthful experiences in dining on wild turkey. "I never tasted domestic turkey," she recalls, "until I went off to college.

When it was served there, I found the dry breast meat a poor excuse for the juicy, flavorful white meat of wild turkeys I was accustomed to eating."

Those familiar with the savory, succulent flavor of the wild turkey will readily identify with Mrs. Carroll's memories. Today their ranks are much larger than was the case a

generation or two ago, thanks to the still-unfolding saga of the wild turkey's comeback. The story, which must rank as one of this century's most significant wildlife restoration successes, has resulted in the big birds once more roaming remote woodlots and farmlands in great numbers. Wildlife biologists across the country have linked hands with the National Wild Turkey Federation to restore turkeys to their original range and far beyond. Today it is possible to hunt wild turkeys in every state but Alaska. This means that the avid outdoorsman, whether he hunts spring gobblers (which is now the standard approach to the sport) or pursues the rich traditions of fall hunting, has realistic expectations of enjoying a sumptuous feast once or twice a year.

The wild turkey certainly deserves special treatment, for it is a special treat. The recipes that follow, along with interspersed tips on preparation covering subjects such as making use of the complete bird and how to handle your prize in the field, should enable you to prepare and present the wild turkey with all the graciousness and grandeur this noble game bird merits.

DEEP-FRIED TURKEY

1. Clean turkey well (as you do for roasting).

2. Thaw turkey completely and pat dry with paper towels.

3. Do not stuff turkey when deep frying.

4. Rub with dry seasonings of your choice. Suggestions are: seasoned salt and pepper, paprika, cayenne pepper, garlic salt, onion salt, Cajun seasonings or Italian seasonings.

5. Turkey may be injected with liquid seasonings (there are syringes available for this purpose). Some possibilities are: hot pepper sauce, Italian salad dressing or liquid Cajun seasonings.

6. Peanut oil is best for deep frying.

7. You need a very large pot (for example, use a 26-quart aluminum pot for a 16-pound turkey). An outdoor cooker is best for this process.

8. To determine how much oil to use, first fill pot with water and place turkey into water. Water should cover turkey without spilling over. Adjust water level as needed. Remove turkey and note water level (or measure water). Dry pot and turkey well before adding oil. It usually takes 3 to 5 gallons of oil.

9. Heat oil to 300 - 350°F (or until nearly smoking).

10. Very carefully and slowly submerge turkey into hot oil.

11. Cook 3½ - 4½ minutes per pound or until meat thermometer registers 180°F. The turkey tends to float when done.

12. A wire coat hanger hooked to the drumsticks is handy for lowering and raising turkey (or use cotton string draped over outside of pot).

13. Be very careful during the lowering and raising of the turkey.

14. Drain turkey well on paper towels.

15. Wrap drained turkey in foil to keep warm.

16. Allow turkey to rest for 15 - 20 minutes before carving.

17. Carve and enjoy this Southern treat.

Roasted Wild Turkey

ROASTED WILD TURKEY

1 medium onion, cut into chunks
2 ribs celery (with leaves), cut into chunks
2 carrots, cut into chunks
1 bay leaf
1-2 tablespoons margarine or olive oil

Place dressed and cleaned wild turkey in enamel roasting pan. Stuff with onion, celery, carrots and bay leaf. Season turkey with salt and black pepper and rub with margarine. Cover, place in oven and cook at 350°F until done. Baste turkey every 20 - 30 minutes.

There are lots of theories and timetables regarding cooking time; however, investing in an instant read meat thermometer takes a lot of worry out of those special holiday meals. Insert a thermometer into the thickest part of the inner thigh, not touching bone. Temperature should reach 180°F. If you prefer a timetable, use the following guidelines:

- up to 6 pounds, 20 - 25 minutes per pound

- 6 to 16 pounds, 15 - 20 minutes per pound

- over 16 pounds, 13 - 15 minutes per pound

- if bird is stuffed, add about 5 minutes per pound

Stuffing: There is a great deal of dispute over the safety of stuffing fowl. The cavities of wild birds do contain bacteria; to be safe, cook dressing separately in a casserole.

Tips: Some people may say that this method is steaming rather than roasting; however, we feel the breast is not as dry and the cooking time is less. The end result of delicious, moist, golden turkey convinced us that this easy method was our favorite.

If you have leftovers, try some of the following recipes for a change of pace: turkey pie, ring of turkey, quesadillas, enchiladas or salads. Your family will never know you are serving leftovers.

BAGGED TURKEY

1 *wild turkey (about 12 pounds)*
  Seasoned salt, as desired
  Black pepper, as desired
2 *ribs celery, cut into chunks*
2 *carrots, cut into chunks*
1 *large onion, cut into chunks*
2 *tablespoons margarine, softened*
1 *oven cooking bag*

Wash and clean turkey in cold water. Pat dry
with paper towels. Sprinkle turkey with salt and
pepper (outside and in cavity). Place vegetables
in cavity. Rub margarine over turkey. Place
turkey in oven cooking bag and close with the
seal provided. Slit bag as directed. Bake at 325°F
for 2 - 3 hours or until turkey reaches 180°F.

*Tip: If you like tender, moist turkey, try an oven cooking
bag. Try this recipe or follow the directions with the
cooking bags. Some bags require a bit of flour (usually
1 tablespoon). Be sure to add the flour if listed with the
bags to prevent the bag from exploding and to aid in
browning the turkey.*

TURKEY SCALLOPINI WITH ASPARAGUS SAUCE

1 *package Knorr béarnaise sauce mix*
3 *tablespoons chopped leeks*
1 *(15-ounce) can asparagus spears*
1 *pound wild turkey breast fillets*
2 *tablespoons butter*
2 *tablespoons olive oil*
1/2 *cup flour*
1/2-1 *cup freshly grated Parmesan cheese*

Prepare béarnaise sauce according to package
directions. Cook leeks in microwave for about
one minute. Chop half of asparagus and add to
sauce along with leeks. Set aside.

Pound turkey fillets with a meat mallet to tenderize. Melt butter in skillet and add olive oil.
Lightly flour breast fillets and brown on each side
until golden brown. Put breasts in shallow
greased 9 x 13-inch casserole. Spread asparagus
sauce over each breast. Sprinkle with Parmesan
cheese and brown lightly under the broiler. Serve
at once. Do not try to cook ahead and reheat.
Serve with wild rice and squash medley.

<u>SERVES 6</u>

*Tip: Remember that wild turkey is unlikely to be as
tender as chicken; however, the pounding does tenderize
it a great deal. The remaining half of asparagus makes
a nice addition to a green salad.*

SUPREME TURKEY STROGANOFF

1 pound boneless wild turkey breast strips
2 tablespoons butter or margarine
1 tablespoon olive oil
1/2 cup chopped onion
2 large garlic cloves, minced
1 (10 1/2-ounce) can cream of chicken soup
1/4 cup Chardonnay or other white wine
1/4 cup water
1 teaspoon beef bouillon granules
2 teaspoons Worcestershire sauce
1/4 teaspoon coarsely ground black pepper
4 tablespoons sour cream

Tenderize turkey strips with meat mallet and cut into 1/4-inch-wide strips. Melt butter and add olive oil. Heat to medium heat and add turkey, onion, and garlic. Sauté until turkey is done and onion is translucent. Add soup, Chardonnay, water, beef bouillon, Worcestershire sauce and pepper. Bring to a boil, reduce heat, cover and simmer for 30 - 45 minutes or until turkey is tender. Add sour cream and stir until heated through. Do not boil. Serve over pasta or rice.

Tip: For a delicious accompaniment, serve fried ripe tomatoes. Coat 1/2-inch-thick slices of ripe tomato with beaten egg. Then coat with a mixture of corn meal, minced fresh basil, and salt. Place 1 tablespoon olive oil in a fry pan and cook tomatoes until golden brown and hot (about 2 - 3 minutes per side).

RANCH TURKEY STRIPS

1 teaspoon of a packet of Ranch Original Dry Salad
   Dressing Mix
2 tablespoons olive oil
1/2 pound wild turkey breast strips

Combine Ranch dressing mix with olive oil. Marinate turkey strips for 15 minutes. Grill for 10 - 12 minutes in fry pan, grilling pan, broiler or outdoor grill. Serve immediately.

SERVES 2

FIELD DRESSING AND GIBLETS

It is generally advisable, and certainly such is the case during the warm weather which typifies spring hunts, to field dress your bird immediately after killing it. To do this, carefully cut a circle around the anal vent, then slice outward and upward below the point of the breast bone until you can insert a hand in the opening. Next run your hand upward into the body cavity until you reach the heart. Take a firm grip and pull. Usually the heart, liver, gizzard and intestines will come away with a single tug. This opens the body cavity and allows cooling to begin.

If you save the giblets (you should), a plastic, resealable bag comes in handy at this point. Store the heart, liver and cleaned gizzard in it. The giblets can be cooked and chopped up for use in gravy or dressing. Alternatively they can be minced to make a delicious pâté.

Wild Turkey

BASIL PASTA AND TURKEY

    4 tablespoons olive oil
    1 tablespoon butter or margarine
    ½ cup chopped onion
    ½ cup sliced fresh mushrooms
    ½ cup slivered almonds
    2 large garlic cloves, minced
    1 pound wild turkey breast, pounded and cut
        into chunks
    ½ cup sun-dried tomatoes (soaked in hot water)
    8 ounces pasta (spaghetti), cooked
  2-3 tablespoons fresh basil, chopped
    1 teaspoon Italian seasoning
    ½ cup freshly grated Parmesan cheese

Place olive oil and butter in a large frying pan. Sauté onion, mushrooms, almonds, garlic and turkey breast chunks. Cook until turkey is no longer pink. Add tomatoes, cooked pasta, basil, Italian seasoning and Parmesan cheese. Stir to mix well. Serve immediately and top with additional freshly grated Parmesan cheese.

SERVES 3

WILD TURKEY TENDERS

    1 egg
    1 tablespoon water
    1 pound wild turkey breast, cut into 1-inch strips
    1 cup all-purpose flour
    ½ cup canola oil
      Salt and black pepper to taste

Beat egg with water. Dredge turkey strips in flour, dip in egg mixture, then again in flour. Fry in canola oil in cast iron skillet until brown and tender. Season with salt and black pepper. Serve immediately.

SERVES 3 - 4

Tip: If turkey is not tender, cover and steam a few minutes after you have browned the strips. The turkey will not be as crisp but the steaming will tenderize if you have a tough bird.

BLACK WALNUT CRUSTED TURKEY

    1 pound wild turkey breast cutlets, pounded with a
        meat mallet
    ½ cup oil-and-vinegar salad dressing
    ⅓ cup finely chopped black walnuts
    ½ cup fresh bread crumbs
    1 tablespoon finely chopped fresh chives
    1 tablespoon margarine
    2 tablespoons olive oil

Place pounded wild turkey breast cutlets in a quart plastic bag. Pour salad dressing over turkey and marinate in the refrigerator for at least 6 hours (or overnight).

Place black walnuts and bread crumbs in blender and process until fine. Add chives.

In large skillet, melt margarine and add olive oil over medium high heat. Drain cutlets and dip into combined black walnuts and bread crumbs; press to coat.

Place turkey cutlets in skillet and reduce heat to medium; cook for 4 to 6 minutes per side until golden brown and the interior is no longer pink. Serve immediately.

SERVES 4

TURKEY TENDERS PARMESAN

      1 egg, beaten
      ½ bottle prepared ranch dressing
  1½-2 cups bread crumbs
   ¼-½ cup Parmesan cheese
   8-10 strips wild turkey breast
      2 tablespoons olive oil

Combine egg with ranch dressing. Mix bread crumbs and Parmesan cheese. Dip turkey strips in dressing/egg mixture. Then dredge in bread-crumb mixture. Heat olive oil in non-stick fry pan. Be sure olive oil is hot before adding strips. Brown turkey on both sides and cook until turkey runs clear. If turkey is not tender enough, cover pan and simmer a few minutes.

SERVES 2

Black Walnut Crusted Turkey

Wild Turkey

PROCESSING YOUR BIRD

Once field dressing of your turkey has been completed, the remaining steps in getting it ready for eating or freezing depend in large measure on your plans for cooking the bird. If you plan on making a traditional roasted turkey, the painstaking process of plucking the turkey is recommended.

For most other types of cooking, skin the turkey. Removing the breast meat involves little more than a few quick, clean cuts with a thin-bladed fillet knife. For turkey tenders or similar dishes, this works quite nicely. While working up the breast, remove as much sinew and gristle as possible. For dark meat, separate the legs and thighs by breaking the joints loose; wings too. A single snip with a pair of game shears will complete the task.

Should you plan to freeze the turkey, cutting it into sections makes storage simpler. This is also the time to cut the breast into sections (cut across the grain) if you eventually intend to cook it in this form. Properly packaged, wild turkey will keep in your freezer for up to a year without appreciable loss of quality.

TASTY TURKEY ENCHILADAS

$1/2$ pound wild turkey breast
2 ribs celery with leaves
1 onion
1 bay leaf
   Peppercorns
1 (10-ounce) package frozen chopped spinach (thaw and drain well, pressing with paper towels)
$1/2$ cup cooked, chopped, onion
8 ounces nonfat plain yogurt
3-4 tablespoons sour cream
2 tablespoons flour
$1/8$-$1/4$ teaspoon cumin
   Salt and black pepper to taste
2 teaspoons to 4 ounces chopped, peeled green chiles (use the amount you prefer)
6 corn tortillas
1 cup grated cheddar cheese

Place wild turkey breast pieces in a saucepan along with celery with leaves, onion, bay leaf, salt and peppercorns to taste. Bring to a boil and reduce heat. Cover and simmer to desired tenderness. Remove from water and cool. Chop into bite-size pieces. You need about $1\frac{1}{2}$ cups chopped turkey.

In a bowl combine chopped turkey, spinach (be sure it is well drained) and cooked onion. In a separate bowl mix yogurt, sour cream, flour, cumin, salt and pepper, and desired amount of chopped chiles. Mix $1/2$ cup of this sauce with spinach/turkey mixture. Set remaining sauce aside.

Soften tortillas by heating them in a microwave between slightly damp paper towels for 40 seconds. Divide filling among the tortillas and roll up each tortilla. Place seam side down, in a baking dish sprayed with cooking spray. Spoon remainder of sauce evenly over tortillas. Top with grated cheese and bake at 350°F for about 25 minutes or until heated through and bubbly.

Serve with salsa and green onions for topping. Chopped fresh tomatoes are a good alternative to the salsa.

Tip: Leftover turkey or dark meat from legs can be substituted for the poached breasts.

TURKEY PARMESAN QUESADILLAS

4 flour tortillas
4 tablespoons marinara sauce, divided
1 cup leftover cooked wild turkey, cut into slivers
1/2 cup mozzarella cheese, divided
1/2 cup freshly grated Parmesan cheese, divided

Lightly coat cookie sheet with cooking spray. Place 2 tortillas on cookie sheet. Spoon 2 tablespoons of the marinara sauce on each tortilla. Top each with slivered turkey. Sprinkle 1/4 cup of the mozzarella and 1/4 cup of the Parmesan cheese on each tortilla. Top with 2 remaining tortillas. Bake at 400°F for 10 - 15 minutes or until crisp. Cut into wedges and serve immediately.

SERVES 2

WILD TURKEY FAJITAS

1/2 cup soy sauce
1/4 cup olive oil
1/4 cup garlic vinegar (or white balsamic vinegar)
1 garlic clove, minced
1/2 teaspoon (to 1/2 tablespoon) crushed red pepper
    Up to 1/2 teaspoon cayenne pepper
1/2 teaspoon black pepper
1 pound boneless turkey breast strips
1 onion, chopped
1 green bell pepper, chopped
1 red bell pepper, chopped

Combine soy sauce, olive oil, vinegar, garlic, crushed red pepper, cayenne pepper and pepper. Place turkey breast strips in nonaluminum dish along with 1/4 of marinade; refrigerate overnight. In remaining marinade soak chopped vegetables for about 2 hours.

Sauté breast strips and vegetables in a non-stick skillet until turkey is no longer pink in the center. Serve on warm tortillas with sour cream, cheese, salsa, guacamole or toppings of your choice.

Tip: To tenderize, pound the turkey breast with a meat mallet before cutting into strips and placing in marinade.

RING OF TURKEY

1 cup Hellmann's mayonnaise
2 tablespoons Dijon mustard
2 tablespoons chopped fresh parsley
2 tablespoons chopped fresh chives
2 cups cooked chopped wild turkey
2-4 slices bacon, cooked and chopped
1 cup shredded cheese
2 (8-ounce) cans refrigerated crescent rolls

Combine mayonnaise, mustard, parsley and chives and mix well. In a separate bowl, combine turkey and bacon; add cheese and 1/3 cup of the mayonnaise mixture and mix well. Separate crescent rolls into triangles and arrange the triangles in a circle on a round baking stone (or round pizza pan) with wide ends of triangles in the center and points toward the outside. There will be an opening in the center. Place turkey mixture onto widest end of each triangle. Bring points of triangles over filling and tuck under wide end. Filling does not need to be covered completely. Bake at 375°F for 20 - 25 minutes or until golden brown. Serve immediately with the remainder of mayonnaise (for topping) in center of ring.

SERVES 4 - 5

Tips: If you have a pizza baking stone, here is another use for it, but you can use a round pan also.

Try cheese mixtures such as cheddar and Swiss, mozzarella and cheddar, or one of the packaged mixes.

This makes a nice Sunday brunch with curried fruit.

BASIL TURKEY QUESADILLAS

PESTO MAYONNAISE

- 1 large garlic clove, minced
- 1/2 cup slivered almonds and/or pine nuts
- 1 tablespoon butter or margarine
- 1/2 cup packed fresh basil leaves
- 1/3 cup Hellman's light mayonnaise

Sauté garlic and nuts in butter until golden. Place basil, mayonnaise, garlic and nuts in blender. Process until smooth.

- 4 flour tortillas
- Cooking spray
- 1 cup chopped wild turkey
- 1 cup shredded cheese (Mexican blend is nice)

Spray bottom of 2 tortillas with cooking spray. Spread pesto mayonnaise evenly over those 2 tortillas. Top with chopped turkey and shredded cheese. Place remaining 2 tortillas on top of turkey and cheese and spray with cooking spray. Place in non-stick frying pan, covered, and cook until brown. Turn and brown until cheese melts and quesadilla is heated. Serve with thinly sliced red and yellow tomatoes and shredded lettuce on top. Garnish with a dollop of sour cream.

<u>Serves</u> 2

TURKEY FRUIT SALAD

- 1 (20-ounce) can pineapple chunks
- 1 red apple, cored, chopped
- 3 cups cooked rice
- 2 cups cubed, cooked, smoked wild turkey
- 1 cup seedless grapes
- 1/2 cup sliced celery
- 1 (8-ounce) carton light peach yogurt
- 2 tablespoons orange marmalade
- 1 tablespoon grated orange peel
- Lettuce leaves

Combine pineapple, apple, rice, turkey, grapes and celery in a large bowl. Combine yogurt, marmalade and orange peel in a separate bowl, mixing well. Add yogurt mixture to fruit and turkey, tossing to mix. Spoon salad into a bowl lined with lettuce leaves.

<u>Serves</u> 8

TURKEY FLORENTINE PIZZA

- 1 pound wild turkey breast
- 3-4 garlic cloves
- 2 tablespoons olive oil
- 1 teaspoon dried Italian seasoning
- 1 cup (or less) ricotta cheese
- 1/2 cup shredded mozzarella cheese
- 1 (16-ounce) pre-baked pizza crust
- 1 (10-ounce) package frozen spinach, thawed, squeezed dry and patted with paper towels
- 3 tablespoons chopped sun-dried tomatoes marinated in olive oil, drained
- 1/4 cup grated Parmesan cheese

Preheat oven to 425°F. Rinse turkey with cold water and pat dry with paper towels. Pound with a meat mallet. Cut into 1-inch pieces. In large skillet, heat garlic and olive oil. Add turkey and cook for 10 minutes or until done. Stir in seasoning and remove from heat. Combine ricotta and mozzarella; spread on pre-baked pizza crust. Spread spinach over cheese mixture; add turkey and tomatoes. Sprinkle with Parmesan cheese. Bake pizza at 425°F for 12 - 15 minutes or until crust is golden brown and cheese is melted.

<u>Serves</u> 4

TURKEY PIE

- 6 tablespoons butter or margarine, melted
- 6 tablespoons all-purpose flour
- 1/4-1/2 teaspoon freshly ground pepper
- 2 cups homemade turkey broth (or purchased chicken broth)
- 2/3 cup half-and-half or cream
- 2 cups cooked wild turkey, chopped
- Prepared pastry for 2-crust pie (purchased or homemade)

Add flour and seasonings to butter. Cook for 1 minute, stirring constantly. Add broth and half-and-half and cook slowly until thickened. Add turkey and pour into pastry-lined pan. Top with rest of pastry and pinch edges together. Bake at 400°F for 30 - 45 minutes or until pastry is browned.

<u>Serves</u> 6

Tip: Try this simple pie using other game (quail, rabbit, squirrel, duck or venison). This is a delicious way to use leftovers. Add vegetables to make turkey pot pie.

THE MAGIC OF MORELS

Over much of the wild turkey's range, the spring mating season closely coincides with the emergence of morel mushrooms. A warm, soaking spring rain, followed by mild, sunny days, will find these delicacies "popping" along fence rows, at the base of dead or dying elms and other trees and in countless other spots.

A fruitful day of picking mushrooms can go far toward salvaging a day of turkey hunting when not so much as a distant gobble has been heard, while those all-too-rare moments of triumph that find the hunter home from the hill with a glorious gobbler and a bag of morels are occasions long to be remembered.

Morels and wild turkey are a duo of delicacies sure to tempt even the finickiest of palates, and those who enjoy the uneven quest for His Majesty can add a meaningful measure of culinary pleasure to their sporting experiences by hunting the elusive morel as well. Should good fortune shine on your mushroom gathering endeavors, be sure to care for your prize in proper fashion. A brown plastic grocery bag serves quite nicely as a field receptacle. Once you are back home or in hunt camp, rinse the morels in cold water and, if desired, soak for half an hour in a bath of lightly salted water. Morels are best when cooked soon after harvesting, although they will keep reasonably well in a refrigerator for two or three days. If you plan to refrigerate them, remove as much moisture as possible from the rinsed mushrooms prior to storage. This can be done with paper or cloth towels.

Morels have a delicate, slightly nutty flavor, one which lends itself to the similar qualities offered by the breast meat of a wild turkey. Both are at their scrumptious best when prepared in a fashion which emphasizes their flavor rather than masking or overwhelming it. Mushrooms (whether morels or some other edible type) blend in nicely with soups using wild rice and turkey, or they can be a memorable hors d'oeuvre that lays a tasty groundwork for a main course of turkey to follow. Among the recommended ways to prepare morels as an appetizer are sautéing lightly in butter, frying until golden brown after having dipped sliced pieces in beaten eggs and dredging through crumbled saltine crackers, or cooked in a skillet with just enough white wine poured in to avoid sticking. Whatever your preferred means of preparation, serve piping hot.

TURKEYS AND BERRIES

Traditionally, cranberries in either a relish or sauce form have been an accompaniment for wild turkey. Certainly the distinctively tart and pungent taste of cranberries compliments wild turkey quite nicely, but the same is true of a number of other wild berries. For example, raspberries, whether eaten raw or used on biscuits as a preserve, go nicely with one's bird. Much the same is true of blackberries, dewberries and blueberries. A glass of homemade elderberry wine is like nectar as you dine on turkey.

Frequently these wild berries can be found in abundance in turkey terrain, and the shrewd eye will be on the lookout for briars, canes or blooms denoting their presence. A few weeks after the season, their ripening goodness beckons the hunter to return for a few hours' picking and perhaps a bit of scouting to see how the year's turkey hatch came off. Eating a meal of a fairly called and cleanly killed turkey, flanked by a berry dish gathered with your own hands, brings a special kind of satisfaction and gives true meaning to the old adage about "putting meat (and berries) on the table."

TWO WILD SALAD

2	cups cooked wild rice
2	cups cooked white rice
2	cups cooked, diced, wild turkey
1	cup seedless, halved, green grapes
1/2	cup chopped cashew nuts
1	cup chopped tart apple
	Salt to taste
3/4-1	cup mayonnaise (good quality-not salad dressing)

Wild rice and white rice must be chilled or at room temperature. Combine all ingredients and toss gently with mayonnaise to blend thoroughly. Add mayonnaise gradually to avoid adding too much. Chill thoroughly to blend flavors.

<u>SERVES 6 - 8</u>

Tips: Sprinkle chopped apple with Fruit Fresh to prevent darkening. I like to simmer strips of wild turkey breast in water with celery, carrot, onion and peppercorns until turkey becomes tender. You could also use leftover roasted turkey.

This is delicious on a hot summer's day served with an asparagus vinaigrette salad and white wine.

SPINACH STRAWBERRY TURKEY SALAD

8	cups torn fresh spinach
1	cup sliced fresh strawberries
2	cups chopped, cooked, wild turkey
1	cup seedless, halved, grapes
1/2	cup slivered almonds, toasted

DRESSING

2	tablespoons strawberry jam
2	tablespoons white cider vinegar
1/3	cup canola oil

Combine spinach, strawberries, turkey and grapes; set aside. Place jam and vinegar in a blender container; process until blended. Add canola oil gradually (processing constantly). Pour over salad and toss well. Top with toasted almonds. Serve immediately.

<u>SERVES 8</u>

Tip: To toast almonds, place in non-stick frying pan on medium high heat. Stir nuts frequently until lightly browned.

TRIPLE "T" SALAD

1 (10-ounce) package tri-color cheese-filled
　　tortellini (fresh or frozen)
1½ cups cooked, chopped, wild turkey
1 (7-ounce) can garbanzo beans, drained and rinsed
1 cup thinly sliced celery
1 cup peeled, seeded, chopped, fresh tomatoes
¼ cup prepared ranch salad dressing
¼ cup mayonnaise
¼ teaspoon salt, or to taste
¼ teaspoon black pepper, or to taste

Prepare tortellini according to package directions; drain and rinse with cold water. Combine the following in a large bowl: chopped wild turkey, garbanzo beans, celery, tomatoes, ranch dressing, mayonnaise, salt and pepper. Add pasta and mix well. Serve on a bed of lettuce, if desired.

SERVES 6 - 8

Tips: To seed tomatoes, quarter the peeled tomatoes and use the tip of your knife or fingers to remove the seeds and juice. Using unseeded tomatoes in this salad makes the salad too juicy and watery.

When preparing pasta salads, always rinse the cooked pasta under cold water to prevent pasta from becoming gummy. If preparing salad to serve immediately, place cooked pasta in ice water briefly to cool.

TURKEY SPAGHETTI SAUCE

2 tablespoons olive oil
½ cup chopped onion
2 garlic cloves, finely chopped
1 pound wild turkey meat, finely chopped or ground
2 (16-ounce) cans Italian stewed tomatoes
1 (6-ounce) can tomato paste
1 teaspoon dried oregano
1½ teaspoons dried basil
1 cup dry red wine
¼ teaspoon freshly ground black pepper
　　Salt to taste

In a large saucepan, heat olive oil over medium heat. Add onion and cook for about 3 minutes, until soft. Add garlic and cook for 1 minute longer. Add turkey and cook for about 4 minutes, until white. Add tomatoes, tomato paste, oregano, basil, wine, black pepper and salt. Reduce heat and simmer for 1 hour until mixture thickens. Serve over pasta of your choice with freshly grated Parmesan cheese.

SERVES 4

Tip: You can grind the turkey in your food processor.

WILD TURKEY MEATBALLS

For a very different and tasty appetizer, try these meatballs:

> 1½ cup ground wild turkey
> 1 cup finely crumbled cornbread
> ¼ cup finely chopped, toasted hazelnuts
> 1 large rib celery, finely chopped
> 2 tablespoons finely chopped onion (and cooked in a microwave a bit)
> ¼-½ teaspoon Italian seasoning
> ¼ teaspoon salt
> 1 teaspoon dry mustard
> ½ cup chicken broth
> 1 egg, beaten

Place all ingredients except broth and egg in a mixing bowl. Add broth and egg, being careful to mix very well. Preheat oven to 375°F while you form meatballs. Shape into 1-inch balls and place on 15 x 10 x l-inch baking pan which has been sprayed with cooking spray to prevent sticking. Bake at 375°F for 20 - 25 minutes or until meatballs are browned and no longer pink in the center. Meanwhile, place sauce ingredients in large skillet.

SAUCE

> 1 (16-ounce) can whole berry cranberry sauce
> 1 tablespoon brown sugar
> 1 teaspoon Worcestershire sauce
> 1 tablespoon prepared Dijon mustard with horseradish

Bring to a boil over medium heat. Reduce heat to low and simmer for 5 - 10 minutes stirring occasionally. Add meatballs and heat for 5 - 10 more minutes, stirring occasionally. (Meatballs will be heated through and sauce will adhere to meatballs.) Serve as an appetizer in chafing dish or slow cooker.

Tip: Cut turkey into chunks and grind in a food processor. Good kitchen shears (we use Gerber's game shears) make chopping the turkey a much easier task. Also, the food processor is ideal for chopping the cornbread, nuts, celery and onion; however, process them separately from turkey because it takes longer to chop turkey than other ingredients. Toasting hazelnuts enhances flavor.

DILLY TURKEY PATTIES

½ pound ground wild turkey
½ cup finely crumbled cornbread
2 tablespoons chopped onion
1 egg
¼ teaspoon salt
¼ teaspoon black pepper
¼ teaspoon dried parsley
1 teaspoon dried dill weed, divided
2 tablespoons margarine
1 cup chicken broth
1½ teaspoons Dijon mustard

Place chunks of turkey in food processor and process until ground. Add cornbread, onion, egg, salt, pepper, parsley and ½ teaspoon of the dill. Process until all ingredients are chopped finely and mixed well. Shape into patties about ½-inch thick.

Melt margarine in heavy skillet. Place patties in pan and cook over medium heat until cooked through and browned (about 4 - 5 minutes per side). Remove patties to serving dish. Add broth, mustard and remaining ½ teaspoon of the dill to skillet. Stir and cook until liquid has reduced enough to thicken sauce slightly (about 5 minutes). Pour over patties and serve immediately.

YIELDS 5 PATTIES

To beat the squirrels and turkeys to hazelnuts, gather them in the husk in early autumn and let them dry out before removal for cracking. They're perfect for Wild Turkey Meatballs (recipe at left).

MENUS FOR WILD TURKEY

Assorted Raw Vegetables with Dip

Bagged Turkey*

Chestnut Dressing* with Giblet Gravy

Pecan Crunch Sweet Potatoes*

Green Bean and Corn Casserole

Cranberry Sauce with Grand Marnier*

Refrigerator Rolls

Persimmon Pudding* or Pumpkin Pie

Chardonnay Wine or Berry Flavored Tea

♦ ♦ ♦ ♦ ♦ ♦ ♦ ♦ ♦

Shrimp Cocktail

Turkey Scallopini with Asparagus Sauce*

Hazelnut Rice*

Squash Medley

Mixed Greens with Black Walnut Vinaigrette*

Crusty Sour Dough Bread

Fresh Apple Cake

Chablis Wine or Columbian Supreme Coffee

*Recipe included in cookbook

Wild Turkey

UPLAND BIRDS

Upland bird hunting is one of America's most cherished sporting traditions. The image of a pointer etched against an evening sky—holding staunchly on a sundown covey—is an enduring one, and some of our finest outdoor writing has been produced by individuals for whom bird hunting was the ultimate sporting experience. Men such as Robert Ruark, Havilah Babcock, Nash Buckingham, Archibald Rutledge and Burton Spiller come immediately to mind in this context, and it is well worth noting that these writers sang not only the literary but also culinary glories of partridges and pheasants, woodcock and grouse.

One measure of a fine sporting scribe is his ability to make you hungry when describing food, and when the featured fare is upland game, those skills seem to reach their apex. Anyone who has read Ruark's *The Old Man and the Boy*, arguably the finest single book ever written on our great outdoors, will have fond memories of the manner in which he described the dining delights furnished by that five-ounce bundle of feathered dynamite he called "the noble quail." Similarly, Nash Buckingham could positively wax poetic on the glories of a platter of quail flanked by "cathead" biscuits, while Archibald Rutledge's descriptions of plantation game feasts at holidays invariably

included mention of upland game birds.

For all that they have been heralded in literature, however, feathered upland game too often receives short shrift in cookbooks. That is both unfortunate and unfair, for when properly prepared there is nothing more delectable or delightful. My paternal grandfather was of the fixed opinion that "there's nothing finer than properly cooked pottiges" (a generic term he used to describe bobwhite quail), and far be it from me to argue with his thoughts when it comes to game dishes.

No matter where you live, in all likelihood one or more species of upland gamebird is available nearby in relative abundance. Moreover,

several of the recipes that follow invite experimentation with different species. For example, the breasts of doves and woodcock are

quite similar, while a pheasant or grouse, at least when it comes to matters of the table, really amount to little more than oversized quail. Properly prepared, all upland game birds are delectable, and the recipes which follow offer a wide variety of approaches to enjoying this hunter's delight.

CLEANING YOUR BIRDS

Cleaning birds may seem a simple process, yet all too often it is done improperly. The easiest approach is to skin the bird (not to pluck it), although that is not always best. For example, you should always pluck the feathers from a woodcock to avoid dry meat.

To a lesser degree, the same is true of other game birds, especially if they are to be baked or broiled. If you do have the pluck to do your own plucking (and it is a time-consuming chore) our recommendation is to undertake the chore after your birds cool. The feathers come away much easier and the old-fashioned practice of immersion in scalding hot water to loosen feathers really isn't necessary.

Incidentally, speaking of letting the birds cool, you might even want to consider a bit of aging or "hanging," as the Europeans term it, before readying them for cooking. To do this, remove the entrails and hang the birds from their feet in a cool location. This helps tenderize the meat and works particularly well with grouse and pheasants. We do not suggest hanging for several days, such as is common in England, but you might be pleasantly surprised with the results of 48 to 72 hours in a meat cooler.

Along similar lines, it is a good idea when hunting in really hot conditions—which is frequently the case with doves and can be true of quail and some prairie grouse hunts as well—to ice down birds. On a dove shoot, this is easily accomplished by placing the grey-winged speedsters you down in a plastic bag (one from a grocery store will do quite nicely, although a resealable plastic one is even better). Place them on ice at once. Many dove stools actually come equipped with a cooler compartment.

While birds with the skin intact take pride of place in matters of the kitchen, there can be no denying the appeal of taking the shortcut offered by skinning. For example, we almost always skin doves, and the same is true with a really nice batch of quail shot on a preserve hunt. You lose a bit, because the skin is where the fat is found, but a basting brush or a touch of cooking oil can take care of that problem quite nicely.

No matter how you clean birds, make a point of taking extra pains to remove shot and feathers from them. You will lose some meat, but the only thing more unpleasant than chomping down on a feather is biting into a size 7½ shot. Also, use a sharp knife to cut out any badly bloodied or shot up portions.

SMOTHERED QUAIL

6 whole quail
1/2 cup butter
1/4 cup olive oil
2 (10 1/2-ounce) cans chicken with rice soup
1/2 cup sherry

In skillet, brown quail in butter/olive oil mixture. Place quail in casserole dish. Pour soup and sherry into skillet drippings. Heat to boiling and pour over quail. Cover and bake at 350°F for 1 hour.

SERVES 4 - 6

Tip: Serve with additional rice and curried fruit.

LEMON QUAIL

3 tablespoons butter or margarine
  Salt and black pepper to taste
6 whole quail
3 tablespoons all-purpose flour
2 cups chicken broth
  Juice from 1/2 large lemon
1 teaspoon Worcestershire sauce
  Thin lemon slices

Preheat oven to 325°F. Melt butter in heavy skillet. Sprinkle salt and pepper on inside and outside of birds. Brown quail on all sides and place in baking dish. Add flour to remaining drippings and stir constantly until golden. Add broth and stir rapidly with wire whisk until sauce is smooth and thick. Add lemon juice and Worcestershire sauce. Pour mixture over quail; cover and bake until quail are tender (about 45 minutes - 1 hour). Garnish with thinly sliced lemon.

SERVES 4 - 6

QUAIL IN CREAM SAUCE

4 whole quail
3 tablespoons oil
1 small onion, chopped
1 (4-ounce) jar sliced mushrooms
2 cups reduced fat/sodium chicken broth
1 cup sour cream
1 tablespoon cornstarch dissolved in 1/4 cup water
1 teaspoon paprika
  Salt and freshly ground black pepper to taste

Brown quail in hot oil. Remove from pan; add onion and mushrooms and sauté until tender. Add chicken broth and return quail to pan. Simmer for 45 minutes - 1 hour or until tender. Remove quail. Stir in sour cream and cornstarch/water mixture. Add paprika, salt and pepper. Simmer until smooth and thickened. Pour sauce over quail. Serve immediately over rice or noodles.

Tip: Fresh mushrooms may be used if you desire.

BEEFY QUAIL

1 (2 1/2-ounce) package chopped, pressed, cooked beef
6-8 quail
1 cup sour cream
1 (10 3/4-ounce) can cream of mushroom soup

Line greased shallow 1-quart baking dish with chopped beef. Place quail on top of beef. In mixing bowl, combine sour cream and soup; pour over birds. Bake uncovered at 350°F for 1 hour or until birds are tender.

SERVES 6 - 8

Tip: Quail can be wrapped in slices of beef and secured with a toothpick if you desire.

QUAIL WITH CURRANT SAUCE

1/2 stick butter
4 quail, cut into serving pieces
1/2 cup currant jelly
Salt to taste
1 tablespoon brandy, or to taste

Melt butter in heavy skillet. Brown quail slowly. Remove quail. Add currant jelly and stir well while jelly melts. Season with salt to taste. Return birds to pan and baste with sauce. Cover and simmer until quail are tender. Stir brandy into sauce until just heated and serve immediately.

SERVES 2 - 3

Tip: The butter will burn if too hot. If needed, more butter may be added to the sauce. Don't use margarine; the butter does make a difference in this recipe.

GRILLED QUAIL SALAD

4 quail, cut in half lengthwise through breast
1 cup Italian salad dressing

Marinate quail in Italian dressing (we like Paul Newman's Olive Oil and Vinegar) for several hours in refrigerator. Drain well and grill over glowing coals until skin is browned and desired doneness is reached. Alternatively, a grilling pan may be used. Arrange quail on top of Mixed Green Salad and serve with garlic vinaigrette dressing.

MIXED GREEN SALAD

Mesclun mix, Boston lettuce, or your preferred salad mixture
Grated carrots
White mushrooms
Red bell pepper
Cherry tomatoes
Cucumbers
Red onion slices

GARLIC VINAIGRETTE

1 garlic clove, minced
1 teaspoon Dijon mustard
1 tablespoon rice vinegar
1/4 cup heavy cream
4 tablespoons extra virgin olive oil
Several dashes of salt, to taste
Freshly ground black pepper

Place garlic, mustard, vinegar and cream in small bowl. Slowly add olive oil while beating with wire whisk until emulsified; season with salt and pepper.

Arrange lettuce on 4 large plates. Add other salad ingredients arranged in an appealing manner. Top each salad with one quail half and drizzle with garlic vinaigrette. Serve remaining vinaigrette on the side.

SERVES 4 FOR A LIGHT MAIN COURSE

Apple Quail

APPLE QUAIL

1/4 cup flour
1/2 teaspoon salt, or to taste
1/8 teaspoon paprika
6 quail, breasts and legs
2 tablespoons butter
1/4 cup chopped sweet onion
1 tablespoon chopped fresh parsley
1/4 teaspoon dried thyme (or 1/2 teaspoon
    fresh thyme)
1 cup apple juice

Mix flour, salt and paprika; lightly flour quail pieces. Melt butter in heavy frying pan and brown quail. Push quail to one side of pan. Add onion and sauté until tender (add 1 tablespoon more butter if needed to sauté onion). Add parsley, thyme and apple juice. Stir to mix well and spoon juice over quail while bringing all to a boil. Reduce heat, cover and simmer until quail are tender (about 1 hour). Serve quail on a bed of rice with sautéed apples on the side.

Tip: To sauté apples: Melt 3 tablespoons butter in a skillet, add 2 cooking apples (cored and cut into wedges), and sprinkle with 2 tablespoons sugar (more or less depending on how sweet the apples are). Cook, turning often, until apples are lightly browned. Garnish apples with a light sprinkling of cinnamon sugar.

Pheasant in Mushroom Cream Sauce

OREGANO PHEASANT

2 pheasants, cut into serving pieces
All-purpose flour
1/4-1/2 cup butter or margarine
1 (10¾-ounce) can cream of mushroom soup
    with roasted garlic and herbs, undiluted
1 (10¾-ounce) can cream of chicken soup,
    undiluted
1 (4-ounce) can sliced mushrooms, rinsed
    and drained
1/4 teaspoon dried oregano
1/2 teaspoon minced garlic
1/4 cup sour cream
1/2 cup white wine
    Salt and pepper to taste

Dredge pheasant in flour. Meanwhile, melt butter in 9 x 13-inch baking dish in 325°F oven. Place pheasant in dish, cover and bake at 325°F for 1 hour. Combine soups, mushrooms, oregano, garlic, sour cream, wine, salt and pepper. Turn pheasant pieces and pour sauce over pheasant. Bake, uncovered, for 1 hour or until tender.

SERVES 4

PHEASANT IN MUSHROOM CREAM SAUCE

1 pheasant (1½-2 pounds)
1/2 cup onion
1 cup fresh sliced mushrooms
2 tablespoons butter or margarine
3 ounces cream cheese
1 (10¾-ounce) can cream of mushroom soup
1/4 cup water
2 tablespoons milk
1/2 cup shredded carrots
1 tablespoon parsley flakes
1 teaspoon instant chicken bouillon

Salt and pepper pheasant and place in greased baking dish, skin side down. Bake at 350°F for 30 minutes.

Meanwhile, prepare mushroom cream sauce: Sauté onion and mushrooms in butter until tender. Add remaining ingredients and stir until smooth.

After pheasant has baked for 30 minutes, turn pheasant and add mushroom cream sauce. Cover and continue baking until tender. Serve with wild rice.

KAYE'S PHEASANT WITH WILD RICE CASSEROLE

1/2 pound fresh mushrooms, sliced, or 4-ounce can
    mushrooms
2-4 tablespoons butter
1 onion, finely chopped
1 cup finely chopped fresh parsley
1/2 cup chopped celery
1 (10¾-ounce) can cream of mushroom soup
1/2 soup can milk
1 cup grated cheddar cheese
2 cups cooked wild rice
2 pheasants, cut into pieces
    Flour
    Paprika

Cook mushrooms in butter for 5 minutes. Remove mushrooms; add onions, parsley and celery to pan; cook until onions are tender and golden. In separate saucepan, heat soup and milk. Add cheese. Add to wild rice and mushroom mixture. Roll pheasant in flour and brown in shortening. Pour rice mixture into greased casserole. Top with pheasant. Sprinkle with paprika. Cover and bake at 325°F for 1 hour.

Tip: Top with slivered almonds if you wish.

SOUPER PHEASANT

½ cup chopped leeks
1 cup fresh sliced mushrooms
1 garlic clove, minced
1 tablespoon olive oil
1 (10¾-ounce) can cream of mushroom soup
½ cup apple juice or water
1 tablespoon Worcestershire sauce
1 pheasant, quartered
  Paprika

Sauté leeks, mushrooms and garlic in olive oil until tender. Add soup, juice and Worcestershire sauce. Pour over pheasant in baking dish. Sprinkle with paprika. Bake at 350°F uncovered for 1½ - 2 hours. Baste occasionally.

SERVES 2 - 3

PHEASANT BITES

1 pheasant breast, fillet and pound to tenderize and cut into small bites
3-4 tablespoons canola oil

EGG MIXTURE

1 egg, beaten
½ cup milk

CRUMB MIXTURE

1 cup fine bread crumbs
3 tablespoons Parmesan cheese
1 teaspoon garlic salt
1 tablespoon parsley

Dip pheasant bites into egg mixture and then roll in crumb mixture. Fry quickly in canola oil until golden brown. Serve as a appetizer with ranch salad dressing for dipping.

DOVE BREAST APPETIZERS

Dove breasts
Italian salad dressing
Bacon slices, cut in half and precooked a bit in the
  microwave

Marinate dove breasts in your favorite Italian dressing (we like Paul Newman's Olive Oil and Vinegar) for at least 4 hours. Wrap bacon strip around each dove breast and secure each with toothpick. Place on hot grill and cook for approximately 8 - 10 minutes, turning often or until center is pink.

Tip: Optional stuffings for variation: wrap each dove breast around a jalapeño pepper half and onion slice, or water chestnut, or pepper cheese before putting bacon around dove breasts.

LEMON GARLIC DOVES

½ cup butter or margarine
2 tablespoons freshly squeezed lemon juice
2 garlic cloves, minced
1 teaspoon onion salt
1 teaspoon black pepper
1 teaspoon Worcestershire sauce
20 dove breasts, filleted

Melt butter and add lemon juice, garlic, onion salt, pepper and Worcestershire sauce. Place doves in lemon butter and marinate for 10 - 15 minutes. Grill doves on high heat (use a grilling pan; they flame a great deal on a charcoal or gas grill). Turn frequently and baste with lemon butter. Cook to desired doneness. Do not overcook; doves should be pink inside.

<u>SERVES 4 - 6</u>

Tip: Serve with hazelnut rice, green beans and pinot noir. May also be served as an appetizer.

A TIP FOR BREASTING OUT DOVES

A common post-hunt ritual for successful dove shoots is gathering to breast out the birds. Several hunters working as a team, with some of them using game shears to cut off wings, feet and heads, while others skin the birds, can handle scores of doves in fairly short order. With a little extra effort though, adding a third step to this assembly-line process, it is possible to end up with filleted breasts and very little wasted meat. To do this, cut across the top of the skinned breast immediately below the wish bone. Then, holding the breast firmly in one hand, use the index and middle fingers of the other hand to push the meat away from the breast bone. With a bit of practice it will come away readily in a single piece, ready for grilling, stuffing or other uses.

BUTTERMILK DOVES

	Buttermilk to cover doves
8	doves
$1/2$	cup flour
$1/2$	teaspoon salt
$1/2$	teaspoon pepper
$1/2$	cup canola oil

Pour buttermilk over dressed doves and refrigerate for 4 hours. Place flour, salt and pepper in a bag. Add drained doves and toss to cover doves with flour. Place doves in frying pan with hot canola oil and brown quickly. Cover, reduce heat and steam to desired tenderness.

Tip: Some of the brown bits come off while steaming, but the pan drippings make delicious gravy to serve with doves. For the gravy, add 3 tablespoons flour to 3 tablespoons drippings in pan, stir constantly until flour begins to brown; add 1 cup milk and salt and pepper to taste. Continue stirring until gravy has thickened. Serve over doves, rice or hot biscuits.

CAROLINA DOVES

$1/2$	cup flour
	Salt and pepper to taste
16	dove breasts
2	tablespoons butter or margarine
2	tablespoons canola oil

Place flour, salt and pepper in a brown paper bag. Shake doves in bag to coat well. Heat butter and canola oil to medium hot and brown the birds quickly. Turn and brown on all sides. Add enough water to come halfway up on doves. Cover pan and simmer for 1 - $1\frac{1}{2}$ hours or until doves are tender. Remove doves and thicken gravy with flour and water paste (2 tablespoons flour and 2 tablespoons water). Serve with rice, biscuits and greens.

SERVES 4

SWEET AND SOUR DOVES

1	stick margarine, melted
1	cup vinegar
1	teaspoon Worcestershire sauce
1/4-1/2	teaspoon black pepper
	Salt to taste
12-15	doves, cleaned, dressed

Combine melted margarine, vinegar, Worcestershire sauce, pepper and salt. Marinate doves for 15 - 30 minutes and grill. Do not overcook. Serve with apricot sauce for dipping.

Tip: We frequently use a grilling pan instead of firing up the charcoal grill.

APRICOT SAUCE

1	cup apricot preserves
1/4	cup lemon juice
1/4	cup water
2	teaspoons cornstarch
1	tablespoon brown sugar
2	tablespoons brandy

Mix all ingredients except brandy in a small saucepan. Stir to blend and cook until thickened. Add brandy. Serve with dove breasts.

YIELDS 1 1/2 CUPS

Tip: This sauce goes well with other red meats such as venison, duck or goose.

UPLAND GAME BIRDS AND WILD NUTS

Most lovers of game dishes recognize the marvelous marriage created when game birds are served with rice. What is less well known is that nuts can form an equally tasty partnership in a number of recipes. For example, if you have never tried nuts in a green salad, with some leftover pieces of quail or pheasant thrown in for good measure, a real treat awaits you.

Similarly, where a recipe calls for slivered almonds, you might want to try substituting hazelnuts or, if you have the patience to get the nutmeats, hickory nuts. Where rice dishes come into play, try adding a bit of tasty crunch to them by adding some wild nutmeats. You do need to be careful with black walnuts, because their distinctive taste can overwhelm some mild dishes.

GAME BIRD TIDBITS

Typically, the heart, liver and gizzard of upland game birds are discarded during the cleaning process. But for those willing to put in a bit of extra effort, these tidbits offer the potential for some real taste treats. For example, dove or quail hearts saved over the course of an entire season of hunting, then marinated and grilled, are delightful hors d'oeuvres.

Similarly, hearts, livers and gizzards can be cooked, mixed with some boiled egg and onion, run through a blender and then salted and peppered to taste. The result is a nice pâté which can be spread on crackers or toast points and served with pre-dinner drinks.

RICK'S CREOLE DOVES

16-20	dove fillets
1/2-1	stick butter or margarine
	Chef Paul Prudhomme's Creole Seasoning

Quickly sauté dove fillets in butter and sprinkle with Creole seasoning as you cook the doves. Do not overcook. Doves are best if still pink inside. Serve immediately.

Tip: These are a delicious appetizer. You'll find you cannot cook them fast enough for your guests!

ROASTED GROUSE

1	large onion, chopped
1	rib celery, chopped
1	carrot, chopped
1	garlic clove, minced
1	tablespoon olive oil
1	grouse, cleaned and dressed
1/2	teaspoon salt
1/2	teaspoon pepper
1/2	teaspoon paprika
1	teaspoon flour
1	tablespoon margarine

Sauté onion, celery, carrot and garlic in olive oil until wilted. Stuff grouse with vegetable mixture. Place in roasting pan. Sprinkle with salt, pepper, paprika and flour. Dot with margarine. Bake at 400°F for 15 minutes. Reduce heat to 350°F and cook about 40 minutes longer or until tender.

Grouse in Cream Sauce

GROUSE IN CREAM SAUCE

2 grouse
Salt and pepper to taste
1 onion, quartered
1/2 cup diced celery (with leaves)
1/4 cup diced carrots
1 bay leaf
1 cup water

Place grouse in Dutch oven and add remaining ingredients. Simmer 1 1/2 - 2 hours or until tender. Remove birds and cool. Break meat into small pieces and stir into cream sauce.

CREAM SAUCE

1 cup fresh sliced mushrooms
2 tablespoons butter or margarine
1 (10 3/4-ounce) can cream of chicken soup
1/2 cup milk (add more or less to get as thick or thin as you prefer)
Salt and pepper to taste

Sauté mushrooms in butter. Add soup and milk and heat. Stir until smooth. Add grouse pieces and adjust seasonings. Serve over toast, home-made biscuits, or in pastry shells.

Tip: Mushroom soup is an alternative choice. This is a good way to use leftovers also. Try using turkey, quail, pheasant or rabbit.

Upland Birds

GROUSE IN MUSHROOM GRAVY

2	grouse, cut into serving-size pieces
1/4	cup minced onion
1	tablespoon water
2	(10¾-ounce) cans cream of mushroom soup

Place grouse pieces in a casserole. In a separate dish, microwave onion and water for 45 seconds. Sprinkle over grouse. Spoon soup over birds. Bake, covered, at 350°F for about 1 hour 15 minutes or until done.

SERVES 6

WOODCOCK WITH CHARDONNAY

6	woodcock, split down back
1/4	cup flour
	Salt and pepper to taste
2	tablespoons butter or margarine
2	tablespoons canola oil
1/2	cup chardonnay wine
2	tablespoons freshly squeezed lemon juice

Place birds in paper bag with flour seasoned with salt and pepper. Shake gently. Sauté birds in hot melted butter and canola oil mixture until nicely browned. Add wine and lemon juice. Cover and simmer for about 30 - 45 minutes or until birds are tender.

WORCESTERSHIRE WOODCOCK

MARINADE

1/2 cup	Worcestershire sauce
1/4 cup	olive oil
1/4 cup	wine
1	garlic clove, minced

4	woodcock, dressed (or breast fillets and legs)

Mix marinade ingredients and place in a sealable bag. Add woodcock and turn. Marinate in refrigerator for 12 - 24 hours.

3 tablespoons	butter or margarine
1	onion, chopped
1	garlic clove, minced
1 cup	fresh sliced mushrooms

Melt butter; add marinated woodcock, turning often, and cook over medium heat. After cooking for about 5 minutes, add onion, minced garlic and mushrooms. Stir often and turn birds, cooking to medium rare doneness and until mushrooms and onions are tender.

MENUS FOR UPLAND BIRDS

Dove Breast Appetizers*

Smothered Quail*

Herbed Rice*

Creamy Green Pea Salad

Pecan Curried Fruit*

Homemade Honey Wheat Berry Bread

Fresh Blueberry Pie*

Liebfraumilch Wine or French Roast Coffee

✦ ✦ ✦ ✦ ✦ ✦ ✦ ✦ ✦

Rick's Creole Doves*

Kaye's Pheasant with Wild Rice Casserole*

Wilted Spinach with Pine Nuts*

Layered Fruit Salad

Homemade Onion Cheese Bread

Black Walnut Pound Cake with Frosting*

Hot Spiced Tea or Amaretto Coffee

*Recipe included in cookbook

UPLAND GAME

Most sportsmen of my generation cut their sporting teeth on upland game, with the occasional quest for feathered game interspersing more frequent daytime hunting for squirrels and rabbits. Nightfall meant the haunting music of a baying pack of hounds singing their hallelujah chorus while hot on the trail of a 'coon or 'possum. For those with a bent for sharpshooting, long-distance shots at whistle pigs (groundhogs) offered some welcome variety and did farmers a real favor.

Squirrel hunting in particular afforded a real primer in woodsmanship, thanks to the emphasis it placed on skills such as stealth in stalking, keen eyesight and optimum use of the sense of hearing, the ability to read sign, and accurate marksmanship. Interestingly enough, there is nothing more uniquely American in the world of sport than bushytail hunting. The treetop tricksters formed a central item of diet on frontier fare, thanks in part to the fact that squirrels were incredibly abundant during the days when the American chestnut reigned supreme in millions of acres of hardwood forests. Youngsters cut their shooting teeth on squirrels, with a premium being placed

on "barking" them in order to retrieve the lead bullet for recasting. Skills thereby honed to a razor's edge played a key role in turning the tide in the American Revolution, most notably at the Battle of Kings Mountain, and until quite recently squirrel hunting remained the single most popular shooting sport over much of the country.

Two great conservation comeback stories, those associated with the white-tailed deer and wild turkeys, have changed matters dramatically in the modern era. The attention of today's hunter focuses in large measure on deer and other big game along with America's "big game bird," and as

a result, small game gets relatively little attention. Yet the varied approaches to hunting afforded by upland game retain their historical appeal, and anyone who has sampled and savored the fine fare it can offer knows just how delightful it can be on the table.

The recipes that follow focus primarily on rabbits and squirrels, both of which remain plentiful over much of the country. Indeed, in many states wildlife biologists indicate that the most underutilized game animal is the squirrel. Seasons for upland game typically begin before and continue long after those for deer have come and gone, which means added opportunity to enjoy those precious hours afield which all of us cherish. You will also find some other suggestions for non-traditional game dishes involving 'coons, 'possums and even muskrats; and in that regard, be sure to look at the sidebar on "The Trapper and the Table."

One final thought on upland game seems in order before getting down to the vital matter of fine eating. The future of sport lies with youngsters, and there is no finer way to introduce a budding hunter to the joys of the wild world than through small game hunting. Typically, rabbits and squirrels are plentiful, which means a promise of the action so important in catching and maintaining the interest of those with short attention spans. The targets will be challenging and while there's every chance you won't come home with a game bag containing nothing but air, you still have a golden opportunity to teach the ethical values of cleaning and eating what you kill.

The hunting, killing and cleaning are important steps along the hunter's road, but the final, delicious rewards come on the table. What follows is a sampling of recipes that will help you make that last step to scrumptious eating.

ANNA LOU'S SQUIRREL

1-2	squirrels, dressed
	Water to cover squirrel
1	teaspoon baking soda
1-2	tablespoons butter

Place dressed squirrel in large saucepan. Cover with cold water, add soda and heat to boiling. Remove from heat and rinse squirrel well under running water (rubbing to remove soda). Return to pan and cover with fresh water. Bring to a boil, reduce heat and simmer until tender. Place squirrel in baking dish, dot with butter, and bake at 350°F until browned and crusty.

Tip: Use the broth from cooking the squirrel to make delicious gravy. Rabbit can be prepared in this manner also. A pressure cooker is good to use for tenderizing a squirrel or rabbit and works well with this recipe.

HASH BROWN POTATOES WITH SQUIRREL

$1^{1}/_{2}$-2	cups chopped, cooked squirrel
3	medium potatoes (about $1^{1}/_{4}$ pound)
$^{1}/_{3}$	cup bacon drippings or oil
$^{1}/_{4}$-$^{1}/_{2}$	cup finely diced onion
$^{1}/_{2}$	teaspoon salt
	Several dashes freshly ground black pepper

Remove squirrel from bones and chop into small pieces. Peel and coarsely grate potatoes. Put drippings in skillet and heat. Slide potatoes into heated drippings. Sprinkle onion, squirrel, and seasonings over potatoes. Cover and cook moderately fast until potatoes are browned on underside. Stir to blend, turn over, cover and brown on other side. Total cooking time is approximately 10 minutes. Serve immediately.

SERVES 4

Tip: Use kitchen scissors to make chopping the squirrel an easy task. Rabbit or other game can be used. This is a good way to use a few leftovers.

FRIED SQUIRREL

    1 cup flour
    1 teaspoon salt
    1/4-1/2 teaspoon pepper
    1-2 eggs
    1-2 squirrels, cut up
    1/2 cup canola oil

Mix flour, salt and pepper and place in a paper or plastic bag. Beat egg well and place in a shallow dish. Drop squirrel in flour bag, shake to cover well, remove squirrel, and dip in egg mixture. Return squirrel to flour bag and shake to coat well. Repeat with all the squirrel pieces. Heat canola oil in skillet and quickly brown squirrel. Place browned squirrel in roasting pan or baking dish and bake, uncovered, at 250°F for approximately 1½ hours or until squirrel is tender.

CREAMED SQUIRREL

    1/4 cup chopped onion
    1/4 cup chopped green pepper
    1/4 cup chopped celery
    2 tablespoons butter or margarine
    1 cup chicken or squirrel broth
    1 (10¾-ounce) can cream of mushroom soup
    2 squirrels, cooked and chopped
        (See Anna Lou's Squirrel, previous page)
    2 hard-boiled eggs, sliced
        Small can pimiento (optional)
        Paprika

Sauté onion, green pepper and celery in butter until tender. Add broth, mushroom soup, squirrel, chopped boiled eggs (reserve slices of egg for garnish if desired) and pimiento. Heat thoroughly and adjust thickness by adding more broth if needed to thin or flour/water paste to thicken. Serve in puff pastry shells or over toast points, homemade biscuits or rice. Garnish with egg slices and paprika.

SERVES 4 - 6

Tip: Use the broth from cooking the squirrel to give a better flavor. This recipe can be used for other game, such as rabbit, turkey, pheasant or quail, to make an elegant and easy meal from a few leftovers.

DEALING WITH TOUGHNESS

The old squirrels or rangy rabbits hunters sometimes call "ridge runners" have a tendency to be tough, in sharp contrast to the tender meat that falls off the bone of yearlings. With a bit of experience you will be able to distinguish between animals that are tough and those that are not—with squirrels, sexual maturity will almost certainly indicate a degree of toughness but there are several ways to make tough meat more tender.

One is a day's cooking in a crockpot, which will find the meat of even the toughest old boar squirrel falling from the bones. Another, quicker approach is to parboil the meat in a pressure cooker for 30 to 45 minutes. You can do this and then fry, bake, roast or otherwise cook the squirrel in whatever fashion you select.

Squirrel with Lima Beans

SQUIRREL WITH LIMA BEANS

1/4 pound bacon
2 squirrels, dressed and cut into pieces
2 cups dried lima beans, soaked overnight
   Flour, salt and pepper
1 onion, chopped
2 ribs celery, chopped
2 carrots, chopped
1 tablespoon sugar
1 cup okra
3 potatoes, diced
2 cups frozen corn
2 (16-ounce) cans stewed tomatoes
1 bay leaf
   Dash of thyme and parsley
1/2-1 teaspoon crushed red pepper (as desired)

Dredge squirrel pieces in flour mixture. In Dutch oven, fry bacon and remove. Brown squirrels in bacon drippings; cover squirrels, bacon, beans, onion, celery and carrots with boiling water. Simmer for 2 hours. Squirrel meat may be removed from bones at this point if you desire. Add remaining ingredients and simmer for 1 hour longer or until squirrel and vegetables are tender. If desired, thicken with flour and water paste and adjust seasonings.

Serves 6 - 8

SQUIRREL AND BISCUIT-STYLE DUMPLINGS

2 squirrels
2 bay leaves
1 cup chopped onion
1 cup chopped celery
3-4 carrots, chopped
   Salt and pepper to taste
2 cups water

Cut 2 squirrels into serving pieces. Place in a Dutch oven and cover with water. Add bay leaves and simmer for 1 1/2 hours or until squirrels are tender. Skim if necessary. Squirrel may be removed from the bones at this point and returned to stew if you desire. Add onion, celery, carrots, seasonings and water. Cook for 15 - 20 minutes or until vegetables are tender. Increase heat. Heat stew to boiling. Add dumplings and continue cooking as directed below.

DUMPLINGS

1/2 cup milk
1 cup flour
2 teaspoons baking powder
1/2 teaspoon salt

Slowly add milk to dry ingredients. Drop by teaspoons into boiling liquid. Cook for 15 - 20 minutes longer or until dumplings are done in the center.

Serves 4

BACON SQUIRREL OR RABBIT

Strained bacon drippings
2 squirrels (or rabbits), quartered
1/2 cup flour
1/2 teaspoon garlic salt
1/4 teaspoon freshly ground black pepper
1/4 teaspoon paprika
1 1/2-2 cups fine dry bread crumbs
1/2 teaspoon basil (optional)

Cook bacon and strain drippings. Pat squirrel dry with a paper towel. Roll squirrel in flour mixed with garlic salt, pepper and paprika. Dip in bacon drippings and completely moisten. Dredge in bread crumbs seasoned with basil. Place squirrel in baking dish and bake at 375°F for 30 - 45 minutes on one side; turn and bake on other side for 30 - 45 minutes more or until well browned and tender.

SERVES 4

Tip: Since bacon varies so much in the amount of fat, we did not give an amount; however, be sure to have enough drippings to completely moisten each piece so that the bacon flavor is imparted to the meat. The crumbled bacon would be delicious sprinkled on a spinach salad to compliment the Bacon Squirrel or Rabbit.

SQUIRREL (OR RABBIT) BOG

2 squirrels (or 1 rabbit), cut up
Salt to taste
1 medium onion, chopped
2-3 ribs celery, chopped
Pepper to taste
1/2-3/4 pound smoked venison sausage (or kielbasa)
1 cup uncooked long-grain rice

Sprinkle squirrel pieces with salt and place in Dutch oven with enough cold water to cover completely. Add onion, celery and pepper. Bring to a boil; reduce heat, cover and simmer until squirrel is tender and readily separates from the bones. Remove squirrel, saving broth. Let squirrel cool, remove meat from bones.

Measure broth back into pot. (It is not necessary to drain onion and celery.) Add water if necessary to make four cups liquid. Return squirrel to pot. Cut smoked sausage into 1/4-inch slices. Add to pot along with rice; stir. Add more salt and pepper to taste. Bring to a boil, reduce heat, cover and simmer for about 30 minutes or until most of broth is absorbed into rice or until rice grains are fluffy and tender.

SERVES 4 - 6

Tip: This traditional dish from the South Carolina Low Country is versatile, and various types of meat (such as chicken, venison, wild turkey or other game birds) can be used.

SMOTHERED RABBIT

1 rabbit, quartered
Flour
3 tablespoons butter or oil
1 onion, sliced
Salt and paprika
1 cup sour cream

Sauté flour-coated rabbit in butter until it is browned. Cover rabbit with onion slices and sprinkle with salt and paprika. Pour sour cream over rabbit. Cover and simmer for 1 hour or until the rabbit is tender. Serve with rice.

Squirrel (or Rabbit) Bog

Upland Game

Cleaning Tips

There is no game easier to clean than rabbits. The skin pulls away readily, making for easy removal of the entrails. With four snips of good game shears and one slice of a knife to remove the head, all that remains is to rinse the cleaned carcass. If you are on a day-long hunt, even in cold weather, it is a good idea to remove rabbit entrails immediately. This can be readily done with a single knife slit. If desired, save the quite large liver for pâté, being sure to remove the gall bladder. Discard the liver if it shows any sign of discoloration or is marked by yellow spots.

Cleaning squirrels is a bit more demanding, thanks to their tough skin. One of two ways works quite nicely. You can make a slit in the skin atop the back and then carefully work a knife beneath the skin until it has been cut all around the middle of the animal. Then pull the skin back in both directions, clip off the feet and cut off the head. Finally, remove the entrails and, with mature males, the testicles.

Alternatively, make a slit around the hind legs just above the feet, cut the skin for an inch or so up the hams and pull it over the head. Then remove the entrails. In either instance, if you wish to save the head (many consider squirrel brains a real delicacy), you will need to skin out the head as well. Once the skinning and gutting has been completed, scrape any hair off and quarter the animal if desired. For old squirrels, in particular, it is a good idea to remove the scent kernels from the joint underneath the front legs. For both squirrels and rabbits—and the same is true of 'coons and 'possums—soaking in cold salt water for an hour or so prior to cooking will help remove any vestiges of blood.

RABBIT PIE

  2 rabbits
  1/4 cup butter or margarine
  4 tablespoons flour
     Salt and pepper to taste
  2 tablespoons chopped parsley

Clean and cut rabbits into pieces. Place in saucepan and barely cover with water. Bring to a boil, reduce heat and simmer until tender. Prepare Cream Cheese Pastry (below). Remove rabbit from water, reserving 2 cups broth. Cool rabbit enough to handle. Chop rabbit.

In large saucepan or Dutch oven, melt butter and add flour, stirring constantly. Gradually add reserved broth and stir until thickened. Add salt, pepper, parsley and rabbit. Mix well and stir until thickened.

Pour into pastry-lined deep dish pie plate. Cover with top pastry and cut several slits through top. Bake at 400°F until top is golden brown (about 15 - 20 minutes) and sauce is bubbling.

CREAM CHEESE PASTRY

  1 cup butter or margarine
  6 ounces cream cheese, softened
  2 cups flour

Using mixture, cream together butter and cream cheese. Slowly add flour. Form into 2 balls, wrap in waxed paper and chill for at least 30 minutes before rolling pastry.

Tip: You may like to add onion or a dash or two of hot sauce to the rabbit; however, the simplicity of the pie is very appealing.

The Cream Cheese Pastry is great to use for quiche and will keep in the refrigerator for several days.

This simple pie can be used for other game such as squirrel, turkey, quail or pheasant.

BAKED RABBIT

  2 rabbits, cut into serving-size pieces
  1 cup water
  1/2 cup butter or margarine, melted
     Salt and pepper to taste

Place rabbit in Dutch oven with a small amount of water and simmer until tender. Remove from pan and place in a casserole dish. Pour butter over rabbit and season to taste. Bake at 350°F for 15 - 20 minutes or until golden brown. Gravy can be made from remaining water and pan drippings if desired. Serve immediately.

SERVES 3 - 4

FOIL-COOKED RABBIT

  1 rabbit, cut up
     Rosemary
     Salt and pepper
     Butter
     Celery, chopped
     Carrots, chopped
     Sliced onion
     Worcestershire sauce

Place rabbit on foil. Sprinkle rosemary, salt and pepper on rabbit pieces. Place pats of butter on and around rabbit. Sprinkle with celery, carrots and onion. Shake on a little Worcestershire sauce. Close foil tightly. Bake at 200°F for 3 hours and at 350°F for 1 hour or until tender. Unwrap foil during last 20 minutes of cooking to brown rabbit.

SHERRIED RABBIT WITH POTATOES

¼ cup butter or margarine
¼ cup olive oil
1 rabbit, cut up
2 garlic cloves, minced
1 medium onion, sliced
1 cup tomato juice
¼ cup white vinegar
5-10 drops Tabasco sauce
Salt and pepper to taste
4 medium potatoes, peeled and sliced
½ cup sherry

Heat butter and olive oil in Dutch oven. Brown rabbit. Add all ingredients except potatoes and sherry. Bring to a boil, reduce heat, cover and simmer for 1 hour. Add potatoes and sherry and simmer another 30 minutes or until rabbit and potatoes are tender.

SERVES 4

FRIED RABBIT

1 rabbit
½ cup flour
Salt and pepper to taste
1 egg, beaten
¼ cup milk
Vegetable oil

Cut rabbit into jointed pieces. Season flour with salt and pepper. In separate dish, combine egg and milk. Dip rabbit pieces in seasoned flour, then egg mixture, then flour again. Fry in deep, hot vegetable oil until browned and tender. Drain on paper towels and serve hot. Gravy can be made using some of the pan drippings if desired.

Tip: You must use a young rabbit for it to be tender when fried in this manner.

RABBIT SALAD

2 cups cooked, chopped rabbit
2 cups halved, seedless grapes
1 cup chopped apple
½ cup chopped, toasted pecans
½ cup chopped celery
¼-½ cup creamy cucumber dressing (or mayonnaise)
⅛-¼ teaspoon ground ginger

Lightly mix above ingredients and serve atop cantaloupe and honeydew melon chunks.

THE TRAPPER AND THE TABLE

Most of the recipes in this cookbook focus on the hunter, and understandably so. However, some of us still cling to the slowly dying tradition of trapping, and many of the products of successful trapping lend themselves to table use. Raccoons and opossums are, of course, hunted, but they also regularly end up in traps. Properly handled and prepared, they lend themselves to many of the recipes which are associated with rabbits and squirrels. In the case of 'possums, a time-tested trick is to pen them up for a couple of weeks after they are caught (either while hunting or trapping) and feed them with an eye to eventual table use. My grandfather, who dearly loved 'possum, used to liken this to fattening up hogs for the killing time which came with the first heavy frost.

Also, it is worth mentioning that when hunters take 'coons and 'possums, rather than merely calling the dogs off for another race, they perform a useful bit of game management. Both creatures wreak havoc with a host of ground nesting birds including ducks, quail, wild turkeys, grouse and woodcock by destroying their eggs. Biologists tell me that egg depredation is among the single biggest problem for wild turkeys in many areas. Likewise, it is not an accident that quail, lacking the unpaid gamekeepers (tenant farmers) who kept these preda-

tors in check in days of yesteryear, have seen their populations plummet.

Our point is, quite simply, don't knock it if you haven't tried it. A prime example comes with my boyhood exposure to muskrats. Running a trapline formed an important and treasured part of my adolescence, and that was a time when a prime muskrat pelt could bring $3 or more (a good bit of money for a youngster in the late 1950s). The money from the skins was supplemented by the two bits a neighbor, known to everyone simply as "Aunt Mag," paid for each and every muskrat carcass I brought her.

Aunt Mag always had something simmering in a Dutch oven on her woodburning cook stove, and all a "greedy gut" teenager had to do was mention hunger and she would serve him a bowl of the stew or soup of the day. On one such occasion, a bitterly cold January day, she dished out a thick, delicious stew with chunks of a dark meat swimming amidst potatoes and carrots. After a second, scrumptious bowl, it belatedly occurred to me to ask her what I had been eating. Laughing in her delightful fashion she said, "That be muskrat." That day I learned a valuable lesson thanks to eating meat I probably would never have tried had I known in advance what it was. You might want to consider that lesson as well.

Eating low on the hog

Although none of these recipes deal specifically with groundhog, the flesh of this animal is quite palatable. The diet of this vegetarian closely resembles that of cottontails, and its taste might be described as a cross between rabbit and pork. Groundhogs have a bit more body fat than most wild game, thus avoiding the dryness associated with many animals. It is important to remove the animal's scent kernels and glands during the cleaning process, but the end result can be several pounds of fine, firm meat. If you are one of those who enjoys plinking at whistle pigs using a .223, .22-250 or some other flat-shooting varmint rifle, give the meat a try on the table the next time you have a successful outing. Try substituting groundhog for rabbit or squirrel in any of the dishes which use pieces or chopped up meat, such as "Creamed Squirrel" (page 81) or "Rabbit Pie" (page 87), or roast it as you would 'coon or 'possum.

RED WINE RABBIT

1/4	cup flour
1	teaspoon salt
1/2	teaspoon black pepper
1	rabbit (2 1/2 -3 pounds), cut into serving pieces
3	tablespoons olive oil, divided
1	onion, chopped
1	cup fresh sliced mushrooms
2	garlic cloves, minced
2	teaspoons minced fresh rosemary
1 1/2	cups chicken broth
1	cup dry red wine
2	tablespoons chopped fresh parsley

Place flour, salt and pepper in a paper or plastic bag. Add rabbit, one piece at a time, and toss to coat well. Heat 2 tablespoons of the olive oil until hot (but not smoking) and brown rabbit. Brown rabbit in batches if pan is not large enough. Rabbit will brown more evenly in uncrowded pan. Remove rabbit. Add remaining 1 tablespoon of the olive oil and sauté onion and mushrooms until tender. Stir in garlic and rosemary and stir constantly for about 1 minute. Add broth, wine and rabbit pieces (along with any juices that may have accumulated with rabbit). Simmer covered for 1 hour or until rabbit is tender. Uncover and simmer until sauce is thickened slightly. Add parsley and serve with rice, pasta, orzo or polenta.

SERVES 4

Tip: Rabbit is a good alternative to chicken or pork.

PAPRIKA RABBIT

$1/2$	cup butter or margarine
$1/4$	cup olive oil
1	rabbit, quartered
1	medium onion, chopped
1	medium fresh tomato, peeled and chopped
1	tablespoon paprika
	Salt and pepper to taste
$1/2$	cup water
$1/2$	cup (or more) sour cream

Heat butter and olive oil, and sauté rabbit until brown; remove rabbit from pan. Add onion and tomato to pan and sauté until tender. Add paprika, salt and pepper and stir constantly for about 1 minute. Add water and mix well. Place rabbit back in pan and bring to a boil; reduce heat, cover and simmer. Add water as needed when liquid cooks down and cook until rabbit is tender and only a few tablespoons of liquid remain. Add sour cream and heat to a simmer. (Do not boil.) Serve with pasta or rice.

SERVES 3 - 4

Tip: Rabbit is mild and takes on the flavors of seasonings added. Try this with pheasant also.

CREAMED RABBIT

$1/3$	cup flour
$1/2$	teaspoon salt
$1/2$	teaspoon sage
$1/4$	teaspoon pepper
1	rabbit, cut into serving pieces
2	tablespoons canola oil

WHITE SAUCE

2	tablespoons butter
2	tablespoons flour
$1^{1}/2$-2	cups milk
	Salt and pepper to taste

Mix flour, salt, sage and pepper in a paper bag. Place rabbit in bag and shake to coat thoroughly. Sauté in canola oil until brown. Place rabbit in casserole.

For white sauce, melt butter and add flour. Stir constantly for 1 minute. Add milk. Season to taste and cook until slightly thickened. Pour over rabbit. Bake at 350°F until tender (usually about $1^{1}/2$ - 2 hours).

Upland Game

Lemon Wine Rabbit

LEMON WINE RABBIT

1 rabbit
1 lemon, cut in half
Salt and pepper to taste
2 tablespoons butter, melted
1/2 cup chardonnay wine
1 tablespoon chopped chives
1 tablespoon chopped parsley

Skin and clean rabbit. Rub rabbit with lemon halves and squeeze lemon juice on rabbit. Rub with salt and pepper. Cut rabbit into serving pieces. Brush rabbit with melted butter. Place in roasting pan and bake at 400°F for about 10 minutes. Add wine; reduce heat to 350°F and continue cooking until tender for at least 1 hour until tender. Baste occasionally. Top with herbs. Serve with drippings poured over rabbit. Wine drippings may be thickened with flour and water paste if desired.

ROASTED RACCOON OR OPOSSUM

1	young, whole raccoon or opossum (about 8 pounds)
2	quarts cold water, divided
2	tablespoons salt
1	cup white vinegar
1/4-1/2	pound bacon slices
6	beef bouillon cubes
1	large onion, peeled and quartered

Clean raccoon well. (Be sure all fat and hair are removed.) Combine 1 quart water, salt and vinegar in a large bowl and mix well. Immerse raccoon in vinegar water and wash well. Do not soak. Place raccoon on rack of roasting pan. Place bacon strips across top of raccoon. Add remaining 1 quart water, bouillon cubes and onion to bottom of roasting pan. Cover tightly and bake at 300°F until done. This can take up to 4 hours. When done, the meat will be grayish in color and tender when pricked with a fork. Slice thinly and serve hot.

SERVES 6

Tip: Sweet potatoes compliment 'possum well.

MUSKRAT WITH MUSH-ROOMS AND ONIONS

1	muskrat, cut into serving pieces
1/2	cup flour (seasoned with salt and pepper)
2	tablespoons butter
2	tablespoons olive oil
1	cup sliced onions
1	cup fresh sliced mushrooms
1	(10 3/4-ounce) can cream of mushroom soup

Roll muskrat in seasoned flour and brown in butter and olive oil in Dutch oven. Remove from pan and sauté onions and mushrooms until tender, adding a bit more olive oil if necessary to cook. Add soup; mix well and heat to a simmer. Return muskrat to Dutch oven, cover and simmer until tender.

Tip: Be certain to remove all small scent kernels and glands (particularly those underneath the leg joints). Leaving them intact can impair the flavor of this dish.

MENUS FOR UPLAND GAME

V-8 Juice Cocktail or Bloody Mary

Fried Squirrel*

Baked Sweet Potatoes with Brown Sugar and Cinnamon

Roasted Sesame Asparagus

Gravy

Flaky Homemade Biscuits and Butter

Wild Strawberry Freezer Jam*

Coffee or Tea

✦ ✦ ✦ ✦ ✦ ✦ ✦ ✦

Hot Mulled Cranberry Cider

Rabbit Pie*

Green Peas and Carrot Combo

Pear and Hazelnut Salad*

Homemade Sour Dough Bread

Wild Berry Cobbler with Ice Cream*

Hot Chocolate or Lemon Tea

Recipe included in cookbook

WATERFOWL

In days of yesteryear, there was a time when waterfowl figured prominently on the menus of the finest restaurants in major American cities along the Eastern seaboard and the Mississippi flyway. This was long before passage of the Lacey Act or, for that matter, state or federal game laws. In Chesapeake Bay and in the bayous of Louisiana, in the wetlands of the Carolina coast and in the marshes of the American heartland, skilled market hunters, some of them equipped with punt guns, killed waterfowl in the untold tens of thousands. Even as late as the

World War I era, hunters were regularly taking daily bags of ducks numbering in the dozens. Small wonder, with such wholesale slaughter, that the immortal Nash Buckingham, one of the true "greats" of American waterfowling, could speak of his own youthful hunting excesses as "The Prodigal Years."

Inevitably market hunting, poaching and mindless waste took their toll, and by the time the first federal waterfowl stamp was issued in the mid-1930s, the outlook for ducks was dismal indeed. Thanks to decades of unrelenting efforts, the ducks (or at least most species of them) have

begun to come back, while some species of geese have become so numerous as to pose major threats of destruction of nesting ground habitat. Today the waterfowl picture, while not exactly rosy, is brighter than it has been in a long time.

That means that once more hunters can sit shivering in a blind, listening to the whistling wings of dawn while waiting for the magic moment of legal shooting time to arrive, with a real sense of expectation. Limits have become a bit more liberal and seasons somewhat longer, and today's waterfowler does not have to worry about wearing out the hulls of his shotshells from loading and unloading them.

Instead, chances of coming home with a brace or two of ducks, or maybe even filled limits, are quite good. That means that once again, after the passage of all too many decades, hunters can enjoy not only the wonders of a dawn sky wearing a mantle of pink filled with gabbling ducks; they can also relish the wonderful dishes offered by properly prepared waterfowl.

Orange-Glazed Duck

ORANGE-GLAZED DUCK

1	*wild duck*
1	*teaspoon salt*
½	*teaspoon pepper*
½	*teaspoon paprika*
¼	*teaspoon ginger*
2	*cups orange juice*
1	*teaspoon lemon juice*
1	*tablespoon currant jelly*

Rub cleaned duck with mixture of salt, pepper, paprika and ginger. Place in roasting pan (on a rack) and bake at 400°F for 1 hour. Drain off fat. Pour mixture of orange juice, lemon juice and currant jelly over duck. Baste frequently and continue to bake until tender.

ROAST STUFFED DUCK

1 wild duck, dressed and cleaned
2 tablespoons butter, softened
Salt
Freshly ground black pepper
1 (16-ounce) can sauerkraut
1½ cups water

Rub duck inside and outside with butter and generously sprinkle with salt and pepper. Stuff with sauerkraut. Tie securely with wings and legs close to body. Sear in a roasting pan, breast side up, in 400°F oven for 15 minutes. Add 1½ cups water and baste. Reduce oven temperature to 300°F and cook 30 minutes per pound. Baste often. Add more water if needed.

Tips: People who do not like sauerkraut really like this. A blow torch is a quick and easy way to remove down after dry picking duck.

WRIGHT DUCK WITH STUFFING

1 wild duck
1 teaspoon salt
1 teaspoon oregano
1 teaspoon paprika
½ teaspoon black pepper
¼ cup olive oil
¼ cup lemon juice

Place duck on a rack in roasting pan. Mix above-listed ingredients and pour evenly over duck. Bake covered for 1½ hours at 350°F. Bake uncovered for 30 minutes at 350°F.

STUFFING

1 (14½-ounce) can chicken broth
1 package Knorr vegetable soup mix
3 ribs celery, chopped
1 medium onion, chopped
¾ stick butter or margarine
4 cups herb-seasoned stuffing (any brand)

Place broth and soup mix in saucepan. Heat to boiling and let simmer for 5 minutes. Sauté celery and onion in butter. Mix stuffing with broth mixture and add celery and onion. Serve as a side dish with duck.

SERVES 4

Tip: Wild rice and baked apples go great with this dish.

BARBECUED WRIGHT DUCK

SAUCE

1 cup ketchup
½ cup lemon juice
¼ cup brown sugar
1 tablespoon Worcestershire sauce
½ teaspoon salt
½ teaspoon pepper
½ teaspoon paprika
1 teaspoon hot sauce
2 wild ducks, halved

Mix sauce ingredients in saucepan. Heat to a low boil and simmer for about 5 minutes. Place duck halves on a rack in roasting pan. Spread with barbecue sauce and cover with foil. Bake covered at 325°F for 1½ hours. Remove foil and spoon on remaining sauce. Bake uncovered for 20 more minutes at 375°F.

SERVES 4 - 6

BUCKLEY DUCK

2-4 ducks
Bacon drippings
Salt and pepper
Several garlic cloves, minced
Parsley
Flour
Beef bouillon
Mushroom soup (optional)

Brown ducks quickly in a heavy cast iron skillet using bacon drippings. Remove ducks and cool slightly. If you will use the same skillet for baking in the oven, wipe all fat from skillet. (Duck fat is sometimes strong.) Make a small slit in each side of the duck breasts. Insert into this slit a mixture of salt, pepper, chopped garlic (a lot) and parsley. Then place the ducks in cast iron skillet or Dutch oven with lid. Make gravy using browned flour and beef bouillon and pour over ducks. Cover and bake in oven at 350°F until ducks become tender (approximately 1½ hours). Check ducks periodically for tenderness; sometimes one duck can be removed and another left to cook longer. When ducks are done, remove meat from bones by slicing on either side of breast bone and peeling it away. Put meat back in gravy and serve with rice and Mayhaw jelly. A can of mushroom soup may be added to gravy if you desire.

SERVES 4 - 6

To SKIN OR PLUCK?

The never-ending debate over whether to skin or pluck ducks and geese really has some simple answers. Make your decision on the basis of how much time you are willing to spend in the cleaning process, how you intend to cook the waterfowl, and what you want in the way of self-basting fat for the cooking process.

When it comes to roasting or baking, the cooking process will definitely benefit from the skin being present. It provides some fat that in effect self-bastes the waterfowl as they cook, and the skin also serves to retain moisture and prevent the dryness which can be the bane of wild game cooking.

For grilling, use in stews or gumbos and the like, skinned waterfowl work quite nicely. As for the time factor, skinning certainly expedites the cleaning process, although if you are fortunate enough to have access to one of the machines which remove feathers, plucking may not be necessary.

In the final analysis, the matter is one of personal preference, and waterfowl with or without their skin can be quite tasty.

BAKED DUCK BREASTS

2	duck breasts, filleted into 4 pieces
1½	sticks butter (no substitute)
4	bay leaves
1	tablespoon poultry seasoning
1	tablespoon dried chives (or 3 tablespoons fresh)
1	tablespoon parsley flakes
½	teaspoon garlic salt
	Black pepper to taste
	Dash cinnamon

Fillet the breasts out of 2 ducks and wash thoroughly. Line a baking dish or pan with aluminum foil; leave enough foil to seal when the ingredients are added. Cut butter into chunks and distribute evenly over ducks. Place a bay leaf on each fillet. Sprinkle remaining ingredients on top of the duck breasts. Close foil securely and bake for 1 hour 15 minutes or until tender. Remove bay leaves before serving. Serve with orange sauce.

ORANGE SAUCE

1	cup orange juice
¼	cup sugar
1	teaspoon nutmeg
1	tablespoon cornstarch

In a medium saucepan, combine orange juice, sugar and nutmeg. Bring to a rolling boil, add cornstarch and stir constantly until thickened. Remove from heat.

SERVES 4

Tip: This quick and easy orange sauce is great with duck, goose, turkey, game birds or venison.

DUCK STROGANOFF

    3 tablespoons canola oil
    8 duck breasts, filleted and sliced thinly
    1 medium onion, finely chopped
    3 tablespoons butter
    1 pound fresh sliced mushrooms
    6 tablespoons flour
    2 cups half-and-half or cream
1/2-1 teaspoon salt
  1/4 teaspoon black pepper
  1/8 teaspoon nutmeg
    2 tablespoons white wine
    1 cup sour cream

Heat canola oil in a large skillet over medium heat. Add duck and onion and cook quickly. Duck should still be pink inside. Remove. Add butter and mushrooms and sauté until mushrooms are tender. Remove mushrooms and add flour to pan drippings. Stir constantly for about 1 minute. Add half-and-half, salt, pepper and nutmeg. Stir constantly until thickened. Add duck, onion and mushrooms and simmer briefly to heat through. Add wine and sour cream to hot mixture and heat but do not boil. Serve immediately over wild rice.

SHERRIED DUCK

    2 tablespoons olive oil
    2 tablespoons butter
    4 ducks, halved lengthwise
    3 tablespoons flour
    2 cups chicken broth
1/2 cup sherry
      Salt and pepper to taste

Heat olive oil and butter in a heavy skillet; cook ducks until browned. Place ducks in a 2 1/2-quart casserole. Add flour to pan drippings and lightly brown. Stir in broth and sherry. Season to taste. Pour over ducks, cover and bake at 350°F for 1 hour or until tender.

<u>SERVES 4</u>

Tip: Wild rice complements the duck.

OVEN DUCK OR GOOSE

1/4 cup finely chopped onion
2 tablespoons butter or margarine, melted
1 (10 3/4-ounce) can cream of mushroom soup
4 ounces frozen orange juice concentrate, thawed
1 tablespoon soy sauce
2 tablespoons freshly squeezed lemon juice
1/2 cup red wine
2 ducks, halved or 1 goose, cut up
Salt and pepper to taste

Sauté onion in butter and add to soup, orange juice, soy sauce, lemon juice and wine. Mix together well. Pat ducks or goose dry with a paper towel and sprinkle with salt and pepper. Place birds in roasting pan and pour soup mixture over all. Cover and bake at 300°F for 3 - 3 1/2 hours or until tender. Serve pan juices over birds.

HUNTING DAY CREAMY DUCK

8 duck breasts, skinned and cut into small pieces
Salt and pepper
Small amount of cooking oil
1 medium onion, chopped
2 (10 3/4-ounce) cans cream of mushroom soup
1 (10 3/4-ounce) can beef consommé
1/2-1 cup water
1 teaspoon Worcestershire sauce

Sprinkle duck pieces with salt and pepper and lightly brown in a small amount of oil. Place duck on paper towels to drain. Sauté onions in oil after cooking duck. Meanwhile place remaining ingredients in crockpot and stir well. Add water as needed to make a creamy mixture. (Do not add too much water because the steam from the covered crockpot adds more moisture.) Stir in duck pieces and onion. Cover and cook on low for 6 - 8 hours (or high for 2 - 4 hours). Serve over rice, pasta, toast points or biscuits.

Tip: How delightful to have this ready when you return from a day of hunting.

DUCK APPETIZER STRIPS

Duck breasts, skin removed
Flour
Salt and pepper
1 egg, lightly beaten
1/4 cup milk
Butter

Cut duck breasts into strips approximately 1/2 inch by 3 inches. Season flour with salt and pepper. In separate dish, combine egg and milk. Lightly flour duck strips, dip in milk/egg mixture, and dredge in flour again. Fry in butter until golden brown and crisp. Serve with ranch or honey mustard dressing for a delicious appetizer.

Tip: Try these as an entrée with rice and gravy.

STEVE'S DUCK JERKY

Cut duck into 1/8-inch-thick pieces. For chewier jerky, slice lengthwise along breast.

Marinate duck fillet strips in a mixture that is 1/2 soy sauce, 1/4 Worcestershire sauce, and 1/4 liquid smoke. Marinate over night. Arrange on dehydrator and sprinkle with garlic pepper.

Dehydrate until desired dryness is reached.

APRICOT DUCK APPETIZERS

1/2-1 cup flour
  1/2 teaspoon salt
  1/4 teaspoon black pepper
       Breast from 1 duck, cut into bite-size pieces
    2 tablespoons olive oil
    2 tablespoons butter

Place flour, salt and pepper in a bag. Add duck pieces and shake to coat with seasoned flour. Lightly brown duck in olive oil and butter at medium high heat. Do not overcook. The duck should be pink on the inside. Serve duck immediately with Game Apricot Sauce or your favorite dipping sauce.

GAME APRICOT SAUCE

  1 cup apricot preserves
  1/4 cup freshly squeezed lemon juice
  1/4 cup water
    2 teaspoons cornstarch
  1/4 teaspoon grated lemon peel
    1 tablespoon sugar
    2 tablespoons brandy

Place apricot preserves, lemon juice, water, cornstarch, lemon peel and sugar in a small saucepan. Cook over moderate heat, stirring constantly, until thickened. Remove from heat and add brandy. Serve with duck or goose.

Tip: Try this sauce with venison for a special treat.

GOOSE AND DUCK KABOBS

While venison is commonly used in kabobs, breast meat from geese and ducks, when cut into cubes, will work just as well.

The red meat (which tells the hunter that he is dealing with a bird that prefers to fly rather than walk) can be interspersed with small potatoes, cherry tomatoes or quarters of larger tomatoes, onions, pieces of bell peppers, squash or other vegetables, to make a fine main dish. Keep in mind that some vegetables, especially potatoes and onions, may need some pre-cooking, because with the waterfowl all you want to do is sear the cubes and then cook them to the point of juicy-pink perfection in the middle.

WATERFOWL PÂTÉ

Serious waterfowl hunters, those who take maybe 30 or 40 ducks or a number of geese every season, ought to consider saving the giblets, and certainly the legs, for use in making pâté. Those who enjoy the rich, distinctive taste of liver should save the giblets and cook those of several waterfowl at once. After they are done, cut into pieces and mince or place them in a blender. With the addition of some raw onion, black pepper or capers, you have the makings of a fine hors d'oeuvre. To make things go a bit further, add the meat stripped from the legs.

MUSHROOM STUFFED GOOSE

1	stick butter or margarine
2	onions, chopped
4	slices bacon, chopped
1	pound fresh sliced mushrooms
1	goose
1	cup burgundy wine
	Salt and pepper to taste

Melt half of the butter in a skillet. Add onions and cook for about 3 minutes. Add bacon and cook for 3 more minutes. Add mushrooms and cook for 2 - 3 additional minutes. Stuff goose with mushroom mixture. Place goose in roasting pan. Pour wine over and dot with remaining half of the butter. Season with salt and pepper. Cover and cook at 350°F for 2½ - 3 hours; baste occasionally. Remove lid during last 15 minutes to allow bird to brown. Carve and serve with mushroom stuffing.

ROASTED GOOSE

1 apple, quartered
1 onion, quartered
2 carrots, cut into chunks
2 ribs celery, cut into chunks
1 bay leaf
1 sprig fresh parsley
1 wild goose
1/4 cup flour
1 large oven cooking bag
1 cup chicken broth
1 cup white wine (Sauterne)
   Salt to taste
   Freshly ground black pepper to taste

Place apple, onion, carrots, celery, bay leaf and parsley in the cavity of goose. Close with a small skewer. Pour flour into a large oven cooking bag and shake to coat surfaces of bag. Place bag in a roasting pan and pour broth and wine into bag. Sprinkle goose with salt and pepper and place in bag; close with the tie provided. Cut slits in bag as directed and roast at 375°F for 2 - 2½ hours or until tender. The goose may be browned more by cutting bag and folding back. If you wish to use pan juices for gravy, be sure to remove fat before thickening with flour and water paste. Season gravy with salt and pepper.

Tip: A meat thermometer inserted into fleshy part of the thigh should register 175°F.

Wild rice is a nice accompaniment to goose.

GRILLING DUCK AND GOOSE

The traditional way of cooking a goose and, to a slightly lesser degree, a duck, has been to roast or bake it.

While a stuffed goose or a baked teal wrapped in bacon strips can be sumptuous fare indeed, the faster, simpler approach offered by grilling should not be overlooked. The breasts of ducks and geese in particular lend themselves to grilling. With small ducks such as woodies or teal, you can grill each side of the filleted breast whole. With bigger ducks and geese, along with tundra swans and sandhill cranes (where they can be hunted), some butterflying or division of the breast is recommended. Regular charcoal is fine, but the addition of some hickory chips after the charcoal is glowing will give an even better taste to the fowl.

Make sure the coals are red hot before you start, because with waterfowl as with venison, hot and quick is the way to cook.

GRILLED GOOSE BREAST FILLETS

Goose breast fillets
Red wine (such as Merlot or Burgundy)
1 *garlic clove, minced*
Salt and pepper
Poultry seasoning
Butter

Fillet goose breasts and marinate in red wine and minced garlic. Use enough wine to barely cover breasts. Refrigerate while marinating (4 - 24 hours). Grill breast fillets for 8 - 10 minutes per side, sprinkle with salt, pepper and poultry seasoning, and baste with melted butter while grilling. Slice breasts on diagonal and serve with melted butter.

Tip: These can be grilled in a grilling pan or on a charcoal or gas grill. Use as an appetizer or main course. Do not overcook. Goose should be cooked either rare or medium rare.

GOOSE BREAST IN WINE

1 boneless goose breast, cut in half
½ cup flour
½ teaspoon seasoned salt
⅛ teaspoon garlic powder
¼ teaspoon pepper
¼ teaspoon paprika
3-4 tablespoons olive oil
½ cup white wine (Sauterne or Chardonnay)
½ cup chicken broth or water

Pound breast fillets with a meat mallet to tenderize. Place flour, seasoned salt, garlic powder, pepper and paprika in a bag. Shake breasts in bag to coat with flour mixture. Brown goose slowly in olive oil in a heavy skillet. Pour wine and broth over goose. Cover and simmer until tender.

SERVES 2

ITALIAN GOOSE BREAST APPETIZERS

2 Canada goose breast fillets
Italian salad dressing
Flour
Canola oil

Cut breast fillets across the grain into ½-inch slices. Then cut into 1-inch lengths. Place goose pieces in sealable plastic bag and cover with your favorite Italian dressing. Marinate for at least 3 - 4 hours or overnight. Drain goose well and dredge in flour. Cook in a small amount of hot canola oil until golden brown (about 4 minutes per side). Do not overcook. Drain well on paper towels and serve as an appetizer.

MENUS FOR WATERFOWL

Toasted Pecans*

Wright Wild Duck with Stuffing*

Wild Rice

Orange Glazed Apples

Watercress Salad with Parmesan
Mustard Dressing*

Homemade Garden Herb Bread

Vanilla Ice Cream with Wild
Raspberry Sauce*

Merlot Wine or Iced Tea

✦ ✦ ✦ ✦ ✦ ✦ ✦ ✦ ✦

Apricot Duck Appetizers*

Roasted Goose*

Oven Baked Brown Rice with
Wild Mushrooms

Green Beans with Hazelnuts*

Blueberry Salad*

Homemade Cracked Wheat Bread

Brownie Cake

Raspberry Tea or Coffee

*Recipe included in cookbook

SOUPS, STEWS & CHILI

Whether the setting is the family kitchen, a remote cabin or a tent camp, there is something special about sitting down to a hearty meal that features piping hot soup, stew or chili. Dishes of this type lend themselves to reheating or to situations where a crockpot can be set to simmering at dawn as the hunter takes to the field, secure in the knowledge that upon his dog-tired return at day's end, sustaining fare awaits him. Another great virtue of dishes of this type is that they are ideally suited to utilizing leftovers, inferior cuts of meat, or to the creation of what old-timers in the North Carolina mountains used to call slumgullion: You simply take what is available, add some vegetables, stock or chili powder and eureka, a tasty dish is the result.

While the recipes below are ones that work for us, honesty compels us to admit that many are in greater or lesser degree the product of happen-

stance or chance. Throw in a bit of this or that, always remembering that one or more game meats form the basis upon which you build, season and sample, and before long you have a dish no king would disdain.

Experimentation is one of the never-ending delights of game cookery, and nowhere does it come into fuller play than with soups, stews, and chili. In that context, we would encourage you to consider the two dozen recipes that follow as a starting point which invites expansion as you test them and plow new ground based on your own personal preferences in terms of seasonings, how hot you like your chili, and the like.

Soups, Stews and Chili

TURKEY AND WILD RICE SOUP

6 tablespoons butter or margarine
1/2 cup chopped onion
1 cup chopped celery
1/2 cup chopped carrots
1/2 cup sliced fresh mushrooms
6 tablespoons flour
Salt and pepper to taste
2 (10¾-ounce each) cans chicken broth
4 cups milk
2 cups cooked wild rice
2 cups cubed, cooked turkey (I like to use half dark meat and half white meat)

Melt butter in a large pan. Sauté onions, celery, carrots and mushrooms until tender crisp. Stir in flour, salt and pepper. Add chicken broth and milk. Stir until thickened. Add wild rice and turkey. Adjust seasonings. Simmer until heated through.

SERVES 8

Tip: This is a great way to use the dark wild turkey meat and really adds to the flavor of the soup. Since we like to reserve the wild turkey breasts for very special recipes, our preference is to use cooked chicken breasts along with the dark turkey meat. We prefer the true wild rice, which we order from Minnesota, over the typical kinds seen in most grocery stores. The flavor is superb. There is even a broken wild rice which can be used for soups and is less expensive.

HOME STYLE WILD TURKEY NOODLE SOUP

1 quart homemade stock (see tip under Savory Spinach Turkey Soup, this page)
1 rib celery, finely chopped
1 large carrot, finely chopped
1/4 cup finely chopped onion
1 cup chopped leftover wild turkey
1/4 pound thin spaghetti noodles, broken
Salt and pepper to taste

Remove fat from broth. Bring to a boil; add vegetables and cook until vegetables are tender (5 - 8 minutes). Add turkey and noodles and cook until pasta is al denté. Stir several times to keep pasta from sticking together. Salt and pepper to taste.

SAVORY SPINACH TURKEY SOUP

2 tablespoons olive oil
1/2 cup chopped onion
2 large garlic cloves, minced
2 cups peeled, chopped fresh tomatoes (canned tomatoes can be used if fresh tomatoes are not available)
4 cups turkey stock (see tip)
1/2 cup quick cooking barley
1 (16-ounce) can red kidney beans, drained and rinsed
2 cups cooked, finely chopped, wild turkey dark meat
5 ounces washed, chopped fresh spinach
2 tablespoons chopped fresh basil
Salt and black pepper to taste (we prefer lots of pepper)

Place olive oil in a Dutch oven and sauté onion and garlic until tender but not brown. Add garlic after onions have cooked a bit to prevent garlic from getting too brown. Add tomatoes and simmer for 5 - 10 minutes. Add turkey stock and heat to boiling. Add barley and simmer for 10 minutes. Add kidney beans and dark turkey bits. Heat to boiling and add spinach and basil. Adjust seasonings and cook for 2 - 5 minutes until spinach is tender.

Tips: To prepare turkey and stock place legs, thighs and neck of wild turkey in a Dutch oven. Cover with water. Add 1 medium onion (chopped), 2 ribs celery (chopped), 2 carrots (chopped), 2 bay leaves, salt and pepper. Bring to a boil, cover and simmer until turkey is tender. Remove turkey and cool. Chop turkey finely and remove gristle, skin and any fat. The dark meat makes a thick broth. We like to strain it twice to remove vegetables and bits of bone and foam. This stock is delicious for soups and casseroles. Canned broth is very high in sodium and preparing your own is an easy way to control salt intake.

Many turkey hunters save only the white breast meat, but sound ethics dictate using all edible portions of the bird. This tasty method utilizes the dark meat.

Savory Spinach Turkey Soup

AFTER THE FEAST SOUP

1 turkey carcass
1 large peeled and quartered onion
4 ribs celery with leaves, chopped
1 large carrot, scrubbed and cut into fourths
2 whole cloves garlic
1 bay leaf
    Water to cover

Remove skin from turkey carcass. Put turkey into stock pot and surround with onion, celery, carrot, garlic and bay leaf. Cover with water. Bring to a boil, reduce heat and simmer, covered, for 2 hours. Refrigerate turkey stock and remove fat that accumulates on top. Remove turkey meat from bones and reserve for soup.

8 cups turkey stock (add canned broth if needed)
2 cups skim milk
4 medium potatoes, peeled and diced
3 carrots, peeled and diced
3 ribs celery, diced
1 cup frozen lima beans
2 ounces small shell pasta
2 cups chopped fresh spinach
1 cup frozen peas
    Turkey meat off carcass
1/4 cup fresh parsley
1/2 teaspoon dried basil
1 teaspoon fresh pepper
    Salt to taste
1 cup evaporated milk
2 tablespoons flour mixed with 4 tablespoons water
    (optional)

Cook turkey stock, milk, potatoes, carrots and celery for 30 minutes. Add lima beans, pasta, spinach, peas, turkey meat, parsley, basil and pepper to the soup and cook for 20 minutes. Remove from heat, season with salt if necessary, and stir in evaporated milk. Return to low heat, stirring often. Do not let soup boil. Thicken with flour/water paste if you want a thicker soup.

SERVES 12

PHEASANT TORTILLA SOUP

1 cup chopped onions
2 teaspoons olive oil
1/2-1 package taco seasoning mix
1 (14 1/2-ounce) can stewed tomatoes
4 cups chicken broth
1 3/4 cup thawed frozen corn
2 cups cooked, chopped, pheasant (leftovers)
3-4 flour or corn tortillas, cut into strips
1/2 cup cheese, grated (try Monterey Jack)

In 5-quart Dutch oven over medium heat, sauté onions in olive oil until tender. Stir in taco seasoning mix, stewed tomatoes, chicken broth, corn and cooked pheasant. Bring to a boil and reduce heat to simmer until corn is tender. Cut tortillas into long strips and lightly brown in small amount of olive oil in a non-stick pan. Place strips in a bowl and add soup. Top soup with grated cheese and serve immediately.

Tip: Adjust the taco seasoning mix to satisfy your tastes. Crushed tortilla chips may be used instead of tortillas. Leftover turkey or quail could also be used in this soup.

DUCK SOUP

1	large or 2 small ducks, cut into small pieces
6-8	cups water
2	ribs celery with leaves, chopped
1	large carrot, shredded
1	large onion, diced
1	teaspoon salt
	Black pepper to taste
6	chicken bouillon cubes
2-3	ounces thin noodles

Place all ingredients except noodles in a large kettle. Bring to a boil. Reduce heat, cover and simmer gently for 2 - 3 hours. Skim if necessary and add more water if soup becomes too thick. Meat may be removed from bones, chopped and added back to the soup at this point. Or let everyone debone as they eat. Add noodles and cook until pasta is done. Serve with crusty French bread for dipping.

PASTA e FAGOLI

1/2	cup chopped onion
2	garlic cloves, minced
1/2	cup chopped celery
1/2	cup grated carrots
2	tablespoons olive oil
1	(14-ounce) can chicken broth
1/2	pound ground venison, browned
2	(14-ounce) cans diced tomatoes
1	(8-ounce) can tomato sauce
1	(16-ounce) can red kidney beans
1	(19-ounce) can white kidney beans (cannellini)
1	cup cooked ziti
1/2	teaspoon black pepper
1	teaspoon parsley
1/2	teaspoon basil
1 1/2	teaspoons Italian seasonings
	Salt to taste

Sauté onion, garlic, celery and carrots in olive oil until tender crisp. Add chicken broth and simmer. Brown ground venison. Add venison, diced tomatoes and tomato sauce. Drain and rinse red and white kidney beans; add to soup. Chop ziti with scissors; add to soup. Add seasonings. Simmer for 20 - 30 minutes.

Yields 4 quarts

Tip: Top with freshly grated Parmesan cheese when served.

Boil them bones

A good way to get soup stock or meat from which to make a scrumptious stew is to boil (or pressure cook) bones until the meat on them is falling-off tender.

For example, many hunters discard the rib cage and neck of deer, yet with a bit of work using a meat saw and some cooking in a stock pot, you can get quite a lot of meat. Similarly, the carcass of a turkey can, after cooking, be picked clean by hand and produce the sort of tidbits which are the making of a good pot of soup. Even in the case of small game, such as rabbits and squirrels, the old adage of "waste not, want not" should be kept in mind.

Soups, Stews and Chili

USING LEFTOVERS

Often there will be some meat left over from a venison roast, stuffed goose, baked turkey or any of countless other game dishes. There are endless ways to make use of such remnants, from cold meat sandwiches to salads or pâtés, but one of the best is to use them in soups or stews.

We make a regular practice of keeping soup containers in the freezer, and any leftovers from game meals go straight into them. When a cold winter day or a prolonged rainy spell seems to cry out for a good pot of soup or a thick stew, all that is necessary to get started is to go to one of these containers in the freezer. It doesn't seem to matter if half a dozen different types of game are in it: When married with some vegetables and a tomato juice base in a big pot, then simmered for a time, the end result is an inviting aroma wafting through the house and calling us to the dinner table.

HERBED WHITE BEAN AND SAUSAGE SOUP

1½	tablespoons olive oil
2	cups chopped onion
1	cup chopped carrots
2	teaspoons minced garlic
1	teaspoon dried basil
1	teaspoon dried thyme
1	teaspoon dried oregano
1	whole bay leaf
2	cups chopped and peeled tomatoes
16	ounces dried navy (or other white) beans (see tip)
6	cups chicken stock (or water and stock)
1	ham hock
½	pound browned, crumbled, bulk venison sausage
1	(10-ounce) package frozen spinach, defrosted and drained
	Salt and pepper to taste

In large soup pot over medium high heat, heat olive oil and sauté onions, carrots and garlic. Add dried herbs and bay leaf and sauté for 1 minute. Add tomatoes, drained navy beans, chicken stock or water, and ham hock. Bring to a boil. Lower heat and simmer until beans are tender (do not let liquid cook away completely; add more liquid if necessary) for about 1½ hours.

Remove ham hock and chop ham. Return chopped ham and browned and crumbled venison sausage to soup. Add spinach and cook for about 1 minute. Adjust salt and pepper. Serve immediately with hot homemade bread or bruschetta.

Tip: Beans can be soaked for 6 - 8 hours or use the quick-soak method: Cover beans with cold water. Bring to a boil; boil for 2 minutes. Cover, remove from heat and let stand for 1 hour. Drain and continue with recipe.

MEATBALL SOUP

1½ pounds ground venison
½ cup fine bread crumbs
1 egg
6 cups beef broth or stock
1 cup sliced carrots
1 cup zucchini, cut into 1-inch chunks
½ cup chopped onion
1 cup chopped celery
⅓ cup long-grain rice
1 teaspoon salt
⅛ teaspoon pepper
2 bay leaves
¼ cup ketchup
2 (14-ounce) cans Italian stewed tomatoes,
   undrained and chopped
1 (8-ounce) can tomato puree

Combine ground venison, bread crumbs and egg; mix well. Shape into 1-inch balls and place ½ inch apart in rectangular baking dish or pan (coated with non-stick spray). Bake for 10-15 minutes at 400°F.

Put remaining ingredients in a 5-quart Dutch oven. Add cooked meatballs. Bring to a boil. Reduce heat; cover and simmer for 1 hour or until vegetables and rice are tender. Top soup with freshly grated cheese when served. Crusty French bread goes nicely with this soup.

Tip: A blender does a good job of making fine bread crumbs.

VEGETABLE AND VENISON SOUP

2 large beef or ham bones
5½ cups water
1 pound venison, cut into chunks
2 (16-ounce) cans diced tomatoes
1 tablespoon salt
1 teaspoon black pepper
1 large onion, chopped
1 tablespoon Worcestershire sauce
5 medium carrots, thinly sliced
6-7 large ribs celery, chopped
5-6 medium potatoes, cubed
1 (20-ounce) package frozen green beans
1 (20-ounce) package frozen corn
1 (10-ounce) package frozen lima beans
½ cup barley
1 teaspoon sugar
½ medium head cabbage, sliced

In large soup pot, place bones, water, venison, tomatoes, salt, pepper and onion. Bring to a boil, reduce heat and simmer for 2 hours or until meat begins to fall apart. Remove soup bones and add all ingredients except cabbage. Cook until potatoes are tender. Add cabbage and cook until cabbage is tender. Serve with homemade cornbread or crusty French bread for a hearty meal.

Y̲IELDS 6 QUARTS

Tip: This soup makes such a large quantity that you may want to freeze several quarts for a quick heat-up dinner on one of those busy, hectic days.

QUICK ITALIAN SOUP

$\frac{1}{2}$ pound ground venison
$\frac{1}{4}$ cup chopped onion
  1 (14-ounce) can Italian stewed tomatoes
  1 (16-ounce) can peeled tomatoes, chopped
  1 (10$\frac{1}{2}$-ounce) can double-rich beef broth
  1 (8-ounce) can mixed vegetables, drained
$\frac{1}{2}$ cup canned kidney beans, drained
  1 (5-ounce) package frozen chopped spinach, defrosted
  1 teaspoon Italian seasoning
$\frac{1}{4}$ teaspoon garlic salt
  1 teaspoon parsley
$\frac{1}{4}$ teaspoon pepper
$\frac{1}{2}$ cup uncooked macaroni noodles

In large saucepan or Dutch oven, brown venison and onion. Add tomatoes, broth, vegetables, beans and seasonings. Bring to a boil; add noodles. Reduce heat to medium and cook for 10 - 15 minutes or until macaroni noodles are done.

<u>Serves 4 - 6</u>

VENISON NOODLE SOUP

  4 cups beef broth
$\frac{1}{4}$-$\frac{1}{2}$ pound egg noodles or spaghetti
  $\frac{1}{2}$ pound ground venison
  2 ribs celery, chopped
  1 small onion, chopped
  2 tablespoons butter or margarine
    Garlic salt to taste
    Salt and pepper to taste
    Chives and Parmesan cheese

Heat broth to boiling and add noodles. In separate pan, brown venison. Sauté celery and onion in butter. When noodles are done, add cooked venison, celery and onion to soup pot. Add garlic salt, salt and pepper to taste. Simmer for 10 - 15 minutes. Garnish with fresh chives and Parmesan.

Tip: Leftover cooked burgers can be chopped and used in the soup.

TACO SOUP

1 pound ground venison
1 garlic clove, minced
1 medium onion, chopped
1 package dry taco mix
1 (15-ounce) can stewed tomatoes
1 (15-ounce) can red kidney beans, drained
1 (16-ounce) can corn, drained
1 (10$\frac{1}{2}$-ounce) can beef broth
3 cups water
  Tortilla chips
  Grated cheese (try the Mexican blend)
  Sour cream

Brown venison, garlic and onion. Add taco mix to venison and follow package instructions. In soup kettle, combine tomatoes, kidney beans, corn, broth and water. Add venison mixture and let simmer for 30 minutes. To serve, divide crumbled tortilla chips among 6 - 8 soup bowls and add soup. Top with grated cheese and a dollop of sour cream.

<u>Serves 6 - 8</u>

QUICK AND EASY RABBIT AND RICE SOUP

1 (14-ounce) can chicken broth
1 cup frozen mixed vegetables
1 cup chopped, cooked, rabbit (leftovers)
1 cup cooked rice
1/2 teaspoon basil
   Salt and pepper to taste

Heat broth to boiling; add frozen vegetables and simmer until tender. Add rabbit, rice, herbs and seasonings. Simmer until heated through.

SERVES 3 - 4

CROCKPOT BRUNSWICK STEW

4 cups chicken broth (we like to use 1 (14-ounce) can of chicken broth plus 2 cups homemade broth)
2-3 cups chopped and cooked chicken, turkey, pheasant, rabbit or squirrel
1 pound cooked and chopped venison
1 (10-ounce) package frozen baby limas
1 (10-ounce) package frozen whole kernel corn
1/2 cup chopped onion
1 (28-ounce) can whole tomatoes, undrained and chopped
2 medium potatoes, peeled and diced
2 tablespoons butter or margarine
1 teaspoon salt
1/8 cup sugar
1/2-1 teaspoon black pepper
1/4 teaspoon red pepper (or to taste)

Place four cups broth in crockpot. Add chopped chicken, turkey or game, chopped venison, and remaining ingredients. Cook on medium for 6 - 8 hours or until potatoes and vegetables are tender.

SERVES 8 - 10

STRETCHING STEW INTO SOUP

When you make a big pot of stew and there is quite a bit left, turn it into even more by taking the soup route.

The process of transition won't quite approach that of the Biblical loaves and fishes, but with the addition of water, stock or tomato juice, you are well on the way from one full meal of stew to another one where soup is the main dish. If you have some extra vegetables to throw in, maybe along with a bouillon cube or leftover meat from a previous game feast, so much the better. Whatever you do, don't throw away extra stew, because today's stew can always be tomorrow's soup.

SQUIRREL AND VENISON STEW

2 squirrels
3-4 chicken pieces (legs or thighs)
1 pound venison, cubed
1 cup sliced celery
1 medium onion, chopped
  Salt and pepper to taste
1 (46-ounce) can tomato juice
1 (10-ounce) package frozen corn
1 (10-ounce) package frozen green beans
4 medium potatoes, cubed
3 carrots, chopped
1 (10-ounce) package frozen green peas

Combine squirrel, chicken, venison, celery, onion, salt and pepper. Cover with water. Cook until meat is almost tender. Add tomato juice, corn, green beans, potatoes, carrots and peas. Cook until tender. Remove bones and serve with hot bread.

SERVES 6 - 8

SQUIRREL BRUNSWICK STEW

2 squirrels, cut up
1½ teaspoons salt
1 onion, minced
2 (10-ounce) packages frozen lima beans
2 (10-ounce) packages frozen corn
½ pound bacon, finely chopped
4 potatoes, peeled and chopped
1 teaspoon pepper
2 teaspoons sugar
2 (14-ounce) cans diced tomatoes
¼ pound butter, cut into walnut-size pieces
  Flour

Cut squirrels into pieces. Heat 4 quarts water to boiling; add salt, onion, beans, corn, bacon, potatoes, pepper and squirrel pieces. Return to a boil, reduce heat, cover and simmer for 2 hours. Add sugar and tomatoes; simmer for an additional hour or until squirrels and vegetables are tender. Ten minutes before completing stew, add butter pieces rolled in flour. (This helps thicken and flavor stew.) Heat to boiling again and adjust seasonings.

PHEASANT PAPRIKASH

2 tablespoons canola oil
1 large onion, chopped
1 large green pepper, sliced (optional)
  Paprika - 1 teaspoon or more (use amount you prefer)
1 large fresh tomato, chopped or 1 (14-ounce) can diced tomatoes
  Few dashes red pepper
  Few dashes black pepper
2 pheasants, cut up
  Salt to taste
2 tablespoons flour
1 cup milk

Place canola oil in Dutch oven and heat. Add onions and sauté until tender. Add green pepper slices and cook for a few minutes. Add enough paprika to make a deep red color and stir constantly for about 1 minute. Add tomato, a few dashes each of red pepper and black pepper. Place pheasant pieces in Dutch oven and add enough water to cover pheasant. Add salt. Bring to a boil, reduce heat, cover and simmer for 2 hours or until pheasant is tender. Mix flour and milk; add to mixture. Adjust seasonings. Let come to a boil but do not boil after adding milk. Serve in bowls over noodles of your choice such as ziti, macaroni or shells.

Tip: Since this is really a cold weather dish, we prefer to use a can of tomatoes instead of the fresh, store-bought tomatoes (which seem to have no flavor in December). Also, when we use canned tomatoes, we add less water and like the richer tomato flavor. Since everyone has to work around the bones, we serve this for a family night dinner with homemade bread and green salad.

SAUERBRATEN

2 pounds venison, cut into chunks
1 (10¾-ounce) can beef broth
⅓ cup packed brown sugar
⅓ cup cider vinegar
½ cup finely chopped onion
¾ cups water
10-12 ginger snaps, crushed

Place all ingredients except ginger snaps in crockpot. Cook on high about 6 hours or until venison is tender. Add crushed ginger snaps and stir until thickened.

CROCKPOT ONION AND GAME STEW

1 pound game chunks (venison, duck, rabbit or
  whatever you prefer)
3-4 medium potatoes, chopped
1 medium onion, chopped
2 carrots, chopped
2 ribs celery, chopped
1 cup sliced fresh mushrooms
1 (10¾-ounce) can onion soup
½ soup can wine
½ soup can water
  Black pepper to taste
1 (5-ounce) package frozen green peas

Place meat, potatoes, onion, carrots, celery and
mushrooms in crockpot and barely cover with
onion soup, wine and water. Cook on medium
for about 6 hours or until meat and vegetables
are tender. Add peas and increase heat to high.
Cook until peas are tender. Thicken stew if
desired with a flour and water paste. Serve with
hot sourdough bread.

SIMPLE OVEN STEW

¼ cup flour
½ teaspoon salt
¼ teaspoon pepper
2 pounds venison stew meat, cut into 1-inch pieces
3-4 tablespoons canola oil
4-5 medium potatoes, peeled and cut into chunks
4-5 carrots, cut into chunks
2 ribs celery, cut into chunks
1 package dry onion soup mix
3 cups water

Mix flour, salt and pepper in a paper bag. Add
venison and shake well. Brown meat in canola
oil and place in large casserole. Add potatoes,
carrots, celery, soup and water. Cover and cook
at 325°F for 2 hours or until meat and vegetables are tender.

THE CHILI CONNECTION

The marvels that chili powder brings
to game are virtually boundless. Chili
can be a main dish, accompanied by
crackers or cornbread and maybe a
salad or piece of fruit, but it can also
be seen as a condiment.

A hot dog or hamburger drenched in
chili to the point where it requires a
fork to eat is one way to get a meal
ready in a hurry, and even teenagers
likely to turn up their noses at more
elaborate fare will dig right in. Or try
adding zest to your chili with raw
onions or green peppers sprinkled
over the top. If you are one of those
hardy souls with a steel-lined stomach
who thinks you aren't eating right
until the food is so spicy you can feel
the heat coming out of the top of
your head, chop up some chili peppers to add zing to the chili powder
you have already used. And of course,
don't overlook the way melted cheese
and chili unite to form a tasty pair.

QUICK AND SIMPLE CHILI

1-2 pounds ground or chopped venison
1 large onion, chopped
1 (14-ounce) can tomatoes, diced
1 (16-ounce) can drained and rinsed beans
  (kidney or pinto)
1 (6-ounce) can tomato paste
1 cup water
1 package chili seasoning
  Salt and pepper to taste

Brown venison and onion. Add tomatoes, beans, tomato paste, water and seasonings. Simmer for 45 minutes or longer for flavors to blend. Serve hot, topped with grated cheese and chives.

Tip: Substitute taco seasoning for chili seasoning and go Mexican with tacos or burritos. Using the pre-packaged seasoning mixes is easy; however, we like to add our own seasonings (chili powder, garlic, red pepper and/or cumin) instead of using a mix. That makes it easy to add only the flavors we like and to adjust the "heat" accordingly.

NORTHERN CHILI

2 pounds ground or chopped venison
2 tablespoons canola oil
1 cup chopped onion
1 (6-ounce) can tomato paste
1 teaspoon cinnamon
1 teaspoon black pepper
1/2 teaspoon cayenne pepper
1/2 teaspoon ground cumin
1/2 teaspoon ground allspice
2 tablespoons Worcestershire sauce
2 teaspoon salt
1 tablespoon vinegar
1 bay leaf
1 cup red wine
3 cups water, divided

In a large kettle brown venison in canola oil with the onion; add tomato paste, cinnamon, black pepper, cayenne, cumin, allspice, Worcestershire sauce, salt, vinegar, bay leaf, wine and 2 cups of the water. Heat mixture to boiling. Simmer, stirring occasionally, for 1 hour; add remaining 1 cup of the water and simmer, stirring occasionally, for 2 hours more. Discard bay leaf before serving.

SERVES 6 - 8

Tip: Some people prefer their chili without beans; this is one to try.

CHILI IN THE CROCKPOT

2 pounds ground (or chopped) venison
1 medium onion, diced
1 cup fresh sliced mushrooms
1 garlic clove, minced
1 bell pepper, chopped (optional)
2 ribs celery, chopped
2 tablespoons canola oil
2 (16-ounce) cans kidney beans, rinsed and drained
2 (16-ounce) cans tomatoes, undrained
1 1/2 tablespoons sugar
1 tablespoon Worcestershire sauce
1 package chili seasonings (or 1 1/2-2 tablespoons chili powder)
1-3 cups water
Salt and pepper to taste

Brown venison, onion, mushrooms, garlic, bell pepper and celery in canola oil. Place in crockpot and add all other ingredients. Mix well; cook on medium for 6 - 8 hours.

MENUS FOR SOUPS, STEWS AND CHILI

Pasta E Fagoli*

Hunter's Green Salad and Dressing

Freshly Baked Garlic Breadsticks

Lemon Chess Pie

Chianti Wine or Summertime Tea

✦ ✦ ✦ ✦ ✦ ✦ ✦ ✦ ✦

Crockpot Onion and Game Stew*

Spinach and Avocado Salad

Hot Herb Bread

Baked Pears topped with
Chocolate Sauce

Tea or Coffee

✦ ✦ ✦ ✦ ✦ ✦ ✦ ✦ ✦

Quick and Simple Chili*

Assorted Crackers and Saltines

Chocolate-Dipped Nuts,*
Mixed Fresh Fruits
and Cheese Platter

Frosty Mugs of Beer or Cider

*Recipe included in cookbook

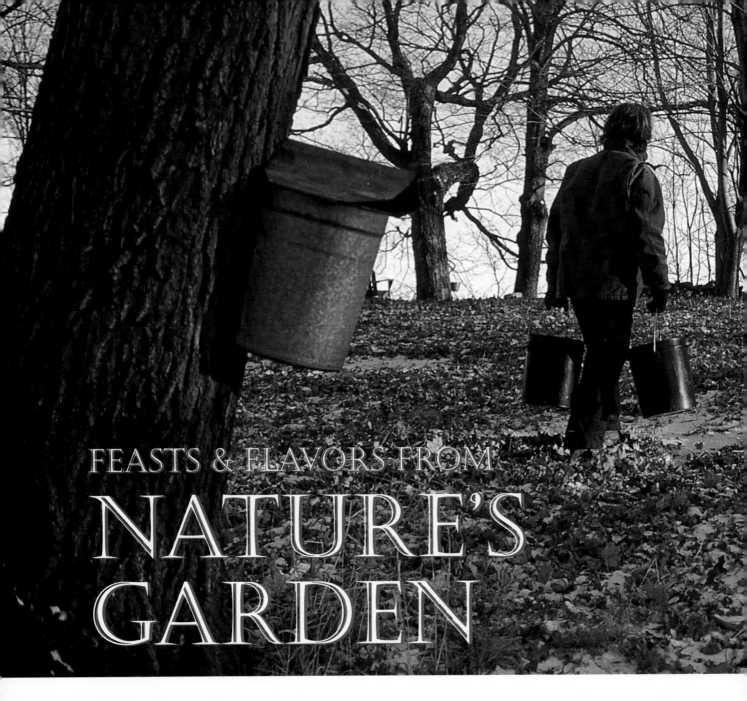

FEASTS & FLAVORS FROM
NATURE'S GARDEN

Man has always been a hunter and a gatherer, and the preceding chapters have focused on the hunting side of our heritage. Historically speaking though, the process of gathering has loomed much larger in man's livelihood through the ages than has hunting. Accordingly, it seems only fitting that we conclude with a selection of recipes that feature some of the incredibly varied bounty available in nature's garden. Wild vegetables, mushrooms, nuts, fruits and berries are our focus here, and throughout the cookbook a special effort has been made to offer recipes where these foods are used in conjunction with meat. Likewise, they figure prominently in the full menus concluding each chapter.

Gathering wild foods can be great family fun, something of an adventure, and a useful connection with the ways of our forefathers.

Moreover, the flavors of the wild often make those of domesticated counterparts seem tame by comparison. No commercially grown strawberries can, for example, match the sweetness and taste of the red jewels found growing in the meadows of spring. Nor can loganberries or garden black-berries come close to matching the taste of those gathered from the wild, with juice-stained hands and a few briar pricks being the honorable signs of work well done.

Any good hunter realizes that consistent suc-cess involves paying his dues in terms of scouting, preseason planning and other aspects of readying one's self for the actual hunt. While the simple process of gathering fruits, nuts, berries and other wild foods

offers its own rewards in the form of fine eating and simple self-satisfaction, there are further rewards to be reaped as well. You may well discover, when picking blackberries, that a particular briar thicket is a favorite bedding place for deer, or an afternoon search for morels just might lead you to a roosting site regularly used by turkeys.

In truth, any time you venture afield there is something to be learned. When Horace Kephart, the author of *Camping and Woodcraft* (and widely hailed as the Dean of American Campers), commented that "in the school of the outdoors there is no graduation day," he surely knew whereof he spoke. In that context, it might also be worth noting that Kephart was an exceptional game cook, as another of his books, *Camp Cookery*, reveals. Take the time to wander through the wilds at all seasons, not merely as a hunter but as a gatherer of food and knowledge. You will soon discover that the process will make you a better hunter and an improved woodsman, not to mention that the efforts will bring new and novel tastes to your table.

WILD STRAWBERRY TRIFLE

1 yellow cake mix, baked according to directions
1 quart wild strawberries (cooked slightly with sugar and a dash or two of Grand Marnier or other orange liqueur)—reserve some fresh berries to decorate top
3 large vanilla pudding mixes (enough for 6 cups of milk), mixed according to directions
2 large whipped topping (24 ounces total)

Cover bottom of large bowl (or trifle dish) with a layer of crumbled cake. Place a layer of strawberries over cake, followed by a layer of pudding and a layer of whipped topping. Repeat layers twice, ending with whipped topping and reserved fresh berries.

SERVES 16

Tip: This is a versatile recipe and works well with other berries. Chocoholics should try this with chocolate cake or brownies, chocolate pudding, and crushed toffee pieces.

WILD STRAWBERRY FREEZER JAM

2 cups crushed wild strawberries
4 cups sugar
1 package fruit pectin
¾ cup water

Combine strawberries and sugar, mixing thoroughly; set aside for 10 minutes and stir occasionally. Mix pectin with water in a small saucepan. Bring to a boil and boil for 1 minute, stirring constantly. Remove from heat, add to fruit and stir constantly for 3 minutes. Pour quickly into sterilized glass or plastic containers with tight-fitting lids. Cover immediately. Let containers stand at room temperature for 24 hours. Place jam in the freezer. Frozen jam may be thawed in a microwave oven. Measurements must be exact for jam to set.

Tip: For raspberries, blueberries or blackberries, use 3 cups crushed berries and 5¼ cups sugar.

WILD STRAWBERRY SPINACH SALAD

4 cups washed and torn spinach
1 cup hulled, rinsed and drained wild strawberries
1 kiwi, peeled and sliced (optional)
⅔ cup chopped macadamia nuts

Combine spinach, strawberries, kiwi and nuts. Set aside.

DRESSING

2 tablespoons strawberry jam
2 tablespoons cider vinegar
⅓ cup oil

Place jam and vinegar in blender and process until blended. Add oil gradually while you continue to process. (This works best if you have a small opening in your blender top to add the oil.) Pour desired amount of dressing over salad and toss gently.

SERVES 4

Tips: If you are fortunate enough to have access to tender dandelion greens, they can be used in place of the spinach.

Try wild raspberries and raspberry jam for a nice change.

A handful of the red jewels that are wild strawberries promises taste beyond compare. As Izaak Walton once said, "Doubtless God could have made a better berry, but doubtless he never did."

STRAWBERRY SECRETS

1. Layer hot pancakes with butter or margarine and fresh wild strawberries with a dusting of powdered sugar.

2. A few wild strawberries add brightness, sweetness and texture to fresh fruit salads or compotes.

3. Add crushed wild strawberries to fresh lemonade or limeade for color and flavor.

4. Drizzle hot chocolate sauce over bowls of fresh wild strawberries for an easy and elegant dessert.

5. Combine 1 pint of wild strawberries with ⅓ cup sugar, ¼ teaspoon rum flavoring and 1 teaspoon fresh lemon juice in blender and purée. Serve over ice cream, pound cake, pudding or custard.

6. Try a few wild strawberries in a glass of champagne.

7. Orange juice, peel or flavoring all compliment wild strawberries.

BERRY CRISP

1	*cup uncooked oats, quick cooking or regular (not instant)*
1	*cup all-purpose flour*
1	*cup packed brown sugar*
1/4-1/2	*cup chopped nuts (walnuts, pecans, or hazelnuts)*
1/2	*cup butter or margarine (cold)*
3	*cups fresh or frozen berries, such as wild strawberries, wild raspberries, wild blackberries, huckleberries or gooseberries*
1/2	*cup sugar (or desired amount)*

Mix oats, flour and brown sugar. Add nuts. Cut in butter or margarine until crumbly. Grease or spray an 8-inch square pan. Place half of crumb mixture on bottom. Mix berries and white sugar and pour over crumb mixture. Top with remaining crumb mixture. Bake at 350°F for 30 - 45 minutes or until golden brown and bubbly. Serve warm with ice cream or whipped cream.

STRAWBERRY BUTTER

1 cup salted butter (at room temperature)
2 teaspoons - 3 tablespoons powdered sugar
¾ cup wild strawberries, hulled, rinsed and drained well

Cut butter into pieces and place in a blender. Pulse until light. Add desired amount of sugar and berries; blend until spread is light and fluffy. Refrigerate in a covered container.

Tip: Here is a recipe that will make a few tasty, wild strawberries go a long way. There are numerous uses for this flavored butter: hot flaky biscuits, croissants, rolls, toast, English muffins, bagels, pancakes or waffles, tea or party sandwiches. Strawberry butter can make a Sunday brunch special.

STRAWBERRY MUFFINS

1 cup self-rising flour
¾ cup sugar
1 egg, beaten
¼ cup milk
¼ cup canola oil
½-1 cup wild strawberries

TOPPING

¼ cup sugar
⅛-¼ teaspoon cinnamon

Using a spoon, mix all muffin ingredients except strawberries until thoroughly mixed. Gently fold in strawberries and fill sprayed muffin tins ⅔ full. Combine sugar and cinnamon and sprinkle over top of muffins. Bake at 375°F for 15 - 20 minutes or until lightly browned. Serve warm with strawberry butter or strawberry cream cheese.

<u>SERVES 12</u>

Tips: This is a great way to "stretch" a small amount of fruit.

Wild strawberries are so sweet that the muffins are like dessert. These muffins are much better served immediately from the oven; they do not reheat well. Blueberries may be substituted for the strawberries.

WILD BERRY COBBLER

1 cup all-purpose flour
1 cup sugar
2 teaspoons baking powder
1 cup milk
¼ cup butter, melted
2-4 cups fresh blackberries, dewberries, elderberries, huckleberries, raspberries, or strawberries

Combine flour, sugar, baking powder and milk; stir with a wire whisk until smooth. Add melted butter and blend. Pour batter into 9 x 13-inch baking dish. Pour berries (amount depends on personal preference) evenly over batter. Do not stir. Bake at 350°F for 30 - 40 minutes or until golden brown. Serve warm with vanilla ice cream, whipped topping or milk.

<u>SERVES 6 - 8</u>

Tip: Leftovers may be reheated in a microwave oven. Sweeten berries if needed.

ELAINE'S BLUEBERRY COBBLER

1/2 stick butter or margarine
4 cups fresh blueberries, rinsed and drained
  (frozen berries may be used, but drain well)
1 teaspoon freshly squeezed lemon juice
3/4-1 cup sugar

TOPPING

1 cup self-rising flour
1 cup sugar
1 teaspoon vanilla flavoring
1/2 cup milk

Preheat oven to 375°F. Melt butter in 8 x 8-inch baking dish in the microwave. Combine blueberries and lemon juice in bowl; add sugar and mix well. Spoon blueberries into baking dish over melted butter; do not stir. Combine flour and sugar in small bowl. Add vanilla to milk and mix into flour and sugar. Pour topping over blueberries and bake for 30 - 45 minutes or until bubbly and golden brown. Serve with whipped cream or vanilla ice cream.

Tip: Try this recipe with blackberries, dewberries or raspberries.

FRESH BLUEBERRY PIE

1 baked 9-inch pie shell (pastry or graham cracker)
4 cups fresh blueberries, divided
1 cup sugar
3 tablespoons cornstarch
1/4 cup water
1/4 teaspoon salt
1/4 teaspoon cinnamon
1 tablespoon butter

Line pie shell with 2 cups of the fresh blueberries. Cook remaining 2 cups of the berries with sugar, cornstarch, water and salt over medium heat until thickened. Remove from heat. Add cinnamon and butter and cool slightly. Pour over berries in shell. Refrigerate. Serve with whipped topping.

EASY BLUEBERRY BUCKLE

4 cups fresh blueberries
1/2 cup maple syrup
1 teaspoon cinnamon
1/4 cup cornstarch
1 1/4 cups flour
3/4 cup brown sugar
1/2 cup butter, softened
1/2 teaspoon almond extract

Gently stir blueberries, maple syrup, cinnamon and cornstarch. Pour into 9-inch square baking dish that has been sprayed. In separate bowl, blend flour and brown sugar. Cut butter and almond extract into flour and sugar until mixture is crumbly. Sprinkle over berries and bake at 375°F for 30 - 45 minutes or until lightly browned and bubbly. Serve warm with ice cream, whipped cream or milk.

SERVES 6

BLUEBERRY SALAD

2 cups frozen or fresh blueberries
1 (6-ounce) package black cherry gelatin
1 cup water
1 (8 1/2-ounce) can crushed pineapple, undrained
1 small carton whipped topping
1 (3-ounce) package cream cheese, softened
1/2 cup finely chopped nuts

Drain blueberries, reserving juice. Add enough water to blueberry juice to make 2 cups. Heat juice to boiling and add gelatin; stir until gelatin is dissolved. Add 1 cup cold water, pineapple and blueberries. Pour into 9 x 13-inch dish and refrigerate until firm.

Beat softened cream cheese, add nuts and fold in whipped topping. Mix well. Spread over congealed salad and chill for at least 2 hours before serving.

Tip: If you use fresh blueberries, place one cup of berries in a saucepan, cover with water and simmer until berries are tender. Drain and continue as directed above but add both the cooked and fresh berries. The contrast in raw and cooked berries is appealing. Huckleberries may be easily substituted in this recipe.

BLUEBERRY BITS

1. Add wild blueberries to your favorite muffin, cake, pancake or waffle batter.

2. Serve your kids a purple cow by whirling milk, wild blueberries and sugar in the blender.

3. Stir wild blueberries into plain yogurt.

Ripe blueberries hang from a bush, awaiting the efforts of a picker.

4. Partially fill an ice cream cone with wild blueberries and top with a scoop of ice cream. Children, and children at heart, will delight in this treat with a surprise at the bottom. For adults, layer wild blueberries and vanilla ice cream in a tall parfait glass.

5. Add wild blueberries to your favorite summer fruits (such as watermelon and cantaloupe).

6. Try a summer ambrosia of wild blueberries, fresh peaches, wild raspberries and pineapple. Add sugar, whipped cream, sour cream or marshmallows. Don't forget the coconut!

7. Layer wild blueberries and vanilla pudding in dessert glasses or a pretty stemmed glass.

8. Try a wild blueberry trifle using a white cake or angel food cake (see the "Wild Strawberry Trifle" recipe, page 122).

9. Try a wild blueberry pizza for dessert. Use a sugar cookie dough, top with sweetened cream cheese blended with whipped topping and a layer of blueberry sauce (cook 2 cups berries and 2/3 cup sugar and thicken with cornstarch/water). Reserve several cups of fresh blueberries for the top.

10. Try a wild blueberry chutney to complement your game dinners.

FINDING BERRIES

One of the easiest ways to locate many types of wild berries is to keep a keen weather eye out for their blooms in the spring. This is especially true of black-berries, dewberries, elderberries and strawberries, all of which sport distinc-tive white blossoms. Look for them along rural roadsides, on farmed-out land, beneath high-power lines and even on the verges of major highways. Fencerows are another likely spot, and the spring turkey hunter who looks for morel mushrooms should also make men-tal notes of the whereabouts of budding or blooming berries. A few weeks later, he can return to pick a luscious feast.

Patches of black raspberries do not offer blooms that are quite so visible, but their purple-hued canes readily catch the eye during late fall and winter. Blueberries, huckleberries, gooseberries and cranberries do not sport particularly distinctive blossoms, but their habitat preferences will help you locate them. All have a distinct preference for acidic soil, and the cranberry requires wetlands to thrive. In most cases, it is possible to return to prime picking patches year after year, as long as the habitat remains little changed.

A vine hangs heavy with ripening blackberries, a promise of luscious treats in the form of jams and jellies, cobblers and pies.

BLACKBERRY DUMPLINGS

1 quart blackberries
1 cup sugar (or to taste)
　Enough water to make berries thin enough to
　　cook dumplings

DUMPLINGS

1 cup flour
2 teaspoons baking powder
1/4 teaspoon salt
1 tablespoon sugar
1 cup milk

Place blackberries, sugar and water in saucepan and heat to boiling. Meanwhile, mix dumpling ingredients thoroughly and drop by tablespoons into boiling berries. Cook for 15 minutes or until dumplings are cooked through the center. Serve hot with cream.

COLD BLACKBERRY SOUP

4 cups rinsed blackberries
1 banana
1 cup sweet pineapple juice
1 cup sour cream
1 tablespoon raspberry liqueur

Place all ingredients in food processor and pulse until blended. Chill. Serve in soup bowls, champagne glasses or tea cups. Serve with toasted pound cake.

Tip: To toast pound cake, cut cake slices with a cookie cutter and place under the broiler until cake is lightly browned. Dip edges of cake in melted chocolate and serve with chilled blackberry soup.

BLACKBERRY SORBET

2 1/2 cups boiling water
1 tea bag (regular size)
3 cups fresh blackberries
1 1/4 cups sugar
1/4 cup freshly squeezed lemon juice (about 1 1/2 lemons)

Pour boiling water over tea bag and steep for 10 minutes. Mix blackberries with sugar. Add tea to the berries; crush berries with the back of a spoon to release juices. Cover and cool. Purée berry/tea mixture in food processor using a metal blade. Divide mixture if necessary. Strain through a fine sieve. Add lemon juice and mix. Refrigerate for at least 1 hour. Place sorbet mixture in ice cream maker and process according to manufacturers' instructions. Freeze sorbet overnight to allow flavors to develop. Makes 1 quart.

YIELDS 1 QUART

WILD BLACKBERRY SAUCE

2 cups blackberries
1/2-3/4 cup sugar
1 tablespoon fresh lemon juice

Mix all ingredients well and refrigerate for 1 hour or more. Allow sauce to come to room temperature before serving. Delicious served over a chocolate tart, cheesecake or ice cream.

WILD RASPBERRY SAUCE

2 cups fresh or frozen wild raspberries
4 tablespoons sugar
1-2 tablespoons Grand Marnier liqueur

Place berries, sugar and liqueur in a small saucepan. Bring to a boil and reduce heat. Simmer for 2 - 3 minutes or until berries are tender. Press through a sieve to remove seeds. Serve over ice cream, cheesecake, pound cake, waffles, French toast or pancakes.

RASPBERRY VINEGAR

½-1 cup raspberries
1 cup white vinegar

Wash berries and drain well. Place fruit in a pretty bottle. Heat vinegar and pour over fruit. Let cool before putting the top on the bottle. Corks are good to use for a top. Keep in a cool place for 7 days before tasting. If you taste the flavor of the fruit, the vinegar is ready. (Set aside for a few more days if you cannot taste the fruit.) You can leave the fruit in the vinegar or strain it out. Store in a cool place.

Tip: Other berries, such as blackberries, blueberries or strawberries, can be used. Flavored vinegars make homemade salad dressings special and are lovely gifts when placed in a special bottle.

HUCKLEBERRY NUT BREAD

¾ cup sugar
½ teaspoon salt
¼ cup butter or margarine, melted
1 egg
2 cups flour
2 teaspoons baking powder
½ teaspoon cinnamon
½ cup milk
1 cup huckleberries (if frozen, thaw and drain well)
½ cup chopped nuts
Cinnamon sugar to taste

Cream sugar, salt and melted butter. Add egg and beat well. In separate bowl, sift flour, baking powder and cinnamon. Add flour mixture to creamed mixture alternately with milk; blend well. Gently fold huckleberries and nuts into batter. Pour into 9 x 5 x 3-inch prepared loaf pan. Sprinkle a very light coating of cinnamon sugar over bread. Bake at 375°F for 45 minutes or until golden brown and bread tests done in center with a toothpick. Cool in pan for 10 minutes before removing.

HUCKLEBERRY PIE WITH HAZELNUT GLAZE

3 cups fresh (or frozen) huckleberries
1 cup grated apple
1 cup sugar
3 tablespoons flour
½ teaspoon almond extract
Several dashes of salt, optional
Pastry for double pie crust
2 tablespoons butter

Mix huckleberries, apple, sugar, flour, almond extract and salt. Pour into unbaked pie shell. Dot with butter. Cover with top crust and bake at 375°F for about 1 hour or until nicely browned. Top with hazelnut glaze when you remove pie from oven.

HAZELNUT GLAZE

⅓ cup packed brown sugar
3 tablespoons light cream
½ cup finely chopped toasted hazelnuts

Place brown sugar and cream in small saucepan over low heat and stir constantly until sugar melts. Stir in hazelnuts. Drizzle over hot pie.

Tip: Try this glaze with blackberry or blueberry pie.

ROSEHIP SYRUP

Place cleaned rosehips in measuring cup. Add an equal amount of sugar and half the amount of water. Cook slowly until rosehips mash easily. Mash with potato masher and press through a sieve. Store in refrigerator and serve over pancakes, waffles, French toast or biscuits.

Tip: Here is another way to get your vitamin C.

Cranberry Sauce with Grand Marnier

CRANBERRY SAUCE WITH GRAND MARNIER

1 cup sugar
1 cup water
3 cups fresh whole cranberries
1-2 tablespoons Grand Marnier or orange-flavored
liqueur

Combine sugar and water in medium saucepan. Cook over medium heat, stirring constantly, until sugar has dissolved and mixture comes to a boil. Add cranberries and return to a boil. Reduce heat and simmer for about 10 minutes. Stir occasionally. Remove from heat and stir in desired amount of liqueur. Chill until serving time.

Tip: Serve with wild turkey and other wild game.

WILD PLUM BUTTER

Wild plums

Water

Sugar

Wash and sort plums. Cut plums in half and pit. Place plums in a heavy-bottomed stainless steel saucepan. Add a very small amount of water—just enough to prevent sticking. Heat plums to a simmer over medium heat; stir constantly. Cook until plums are soft. Remove from heat and press through a sieve. Measure plum pulp and place in a clean, heavy saucepan. Add ¾ cup sugar for each cup of pulp; stir well. Bring sugar and pulp to a simmer over medium heat, stirring constantly. Continue simmering until desired consistency is reached, stirring frequently.

Pour hot plum butter into sterilized jars and seal. Process in hot water bath for 10 minutes for half-pints and for 15 minutes for pints. Remove jars from hot water and place on a dry, folded towel. Let jars stand undisturbed for at least 12 hours to cool completely.

Tip: To test for doneness and proper consistency, place a teaspoonful of hot butter on a plate. If liquid does not run off around the edge of the butter, it is ready.

A handful of ripe wild plums.

WILD CURRANT SYRUP

Wild red currants

Water

Sugar

Wash, sort and clean currants. To extract juice, place currants in large saucepan and mash berries with potato masher. Add enough water to barely cover. Simmer, covered, for about 10 minutes or until juice seems to be extracted. Strain through a jelly bag or cheesecloth. (Do not squeeze bag or juice will be cloudy.) Allow to drain for several hours. Measure out the juice. Add half as much sugar as you have juice and place both in large saucepan. Bring to a boil, reduce heat and simmer for about 30 minutes. Stir occasionally to prevent sticking. This syrup will keep for several weeks in the refrigerator and can be used over pancakes, waffles, French toast or ice cream. Try a bit in lemonade or any other summer cooler.

Tip: Blueberries, raspberries and chokecherries make delicious syrups. Or try combining several kinds of berries for a flavorful syrup. This is an easy way to use a small amount of berries.

PERSIMMON LEATHER

If you have a dehydrator, place one cup of persimmon pulp and ½ cup crushed pineapple in a blender and purée. Spread thinly on plastic wrap or Teflex (our dehydrator has a Teflex sheet to use for fruit leathers) and dehydrate at 135°F until leathery. Average drying time for leathers is 4 - 6 hours. When fruit leather is dry, it will be shiny and non-sticky to the touch. Allow leather to cool and peel from tray. Roll into cylinder shape and wrap with plastic wrap.

Tip: The leather dries more evenly if the purée is ⅛-inch thick at the center and ¼-inch thick at the edges. Don't forget to use your dehydrator for wild berries, fruits and game jerky; they are nice to take on any camping, fishing or hunting trips

UNDERSTANDING PERSIMMONS

Ripe persimmons lie atop fallen sweet gum leaves in late October.

For generations, country boys have enjoyed outwitting their city slicker cousins in connection with the persimmon. As the fruit turns from green to pale yellow then golden orange, it appears to be fully ripe. However, with the persimmon, unlike the situation with many fruits and berries, color is no index to ripeness. One bite from an unripe persimmon will be all that is needed to convince the uninitiated, for its alum-like taste gives an entirely new meaning to the phrase "pucker power."

When ripe though, a persimmon is sugary sweet, so much so in fact that you will have to hustle to beat foxes, 'coons, 'possums, deer and other creatures in harvesting nature's candy. The good news is that you can get a bit of a head start.

Folk wisdom holds that persimmons will not ripen until after the first hard frost, but that is not actually the case. While ripeness does coincide with early frosts over much of the persimmon's range, the fruit can ripen before the first frost or considerably later. When the fruits begin to show wrinkles and drop from trees, they are usually ready for the table. Even if the occasional unripe fruit is gathered at this juncture, there is no problem as long as the persimmons are cooked. Cooking destroys all vestiges of astringency and makes this delightful fruit a sure thing when used in puddings and other dishes.

PEMMICAN: A FOOD FROM THE PAST

Pemmican, a mixture of dried and powdered meat, dried berries and fat, was a staple item of diet for the fabled mountain men, pioneer hunters and early settlers in the American West. It is fun to experiment with making your own pemmican today and using it as a high-energy replacement for gorp or trail mix.

One simple approach is to shred or pulverize some venison jerky, then mix it with dried fruits or berries of your choice. Blueberries, cranberries, chokecherries and huckle-

berries all dry well and can be used in this regard. Blend the meat and berries thoroughly, either by hand or with a blender, then add a bit of shortening to hold the mix together. Butter or margarine can be substituted for the shortening, but the resulting pemmican will not keep well.

Though high in cholesterol, this food takes up little space and will give you the energy for long miles on the trail much as it once sustained the rugged individuals who hunted buffalo and trapped beaver.

Ripening chokecherries, a staple ingredient of traditional pemmican, glisten in the summer sun.

PERSIMMON PUDDING

2 cups persimmon pulp
2 cups packed brown sugar
1/4 cup butter, melted
1 teaspoon vanilla
1 1/2 cups self-rising flour
1/2 cup light cream or milk
2 eggs, beaten
1/2 teaspoon cinnamon
1/2 cup raisins or nuts (optional)

Combine all ingredients and beat just until well mixed. Pour into a greased 9 x 13-inch pan and bake at 350°F for 30 - 35 minutes or until golden brown and just beginning to pull away from the sides. Remove from oven and cool slightly. Cover and seal tightly with foil or plastic wrap. Cut into squares and serve with whipped topping.

Tips: Ripe persimmons are pale orange and very soft with a wrinkled skin. To prepare pulp, rinse persimmons in cold water and press through a non-aluminum sieve to remove the seeds and skin. Then use the pulp or freeze for later use.

Persimmons have a subtle flavor and the spices or flavoring come through more than anything. If you like the flavor of bourbon, a tablespoon may be added to this pudding.

PERSIMMON BUTTER

Wash persimmons thoroughly and remove stems and other debris. Drain well. Press through a non-aluminum sieve to remove skins and seeds. Add honey (to taste) and mix well with a fork. Store in refrigerator. Serve on bagels, muffins, toast or biscuits.

SERVICEBERRY JELLY

6 cups serviceberries
2 cups water
1 package fruit pectin
4 cups sugar
3 tablespoons lemon juice

Place washed berries in saucepan and add water. Bring to a boil and reduce heat. Simmer for 10 - 15 minutes. Pour berries into jelly bag or cheesecloth and let juice drip. Press lightly if needed to make 4 cups juice. Mix juice and pectin; bring to a boil and add sugar and lemon juice. Bring to a hard rolling boil and boil for 1 minute. Remove from heat, skim off foam, and place in sterile jars.

Tip: Serviceberries can also be used in pies.

ELDERBERRY JELLY

JUICE FOR JELLY

6 quarts or 3 pounds elderberries

Wash berries and remove stems. Place in a saucepan and crush some of the berries. Bring to a boil slowly until juice starts to flow. Reduce heat, cover and simmer for 15 minutes. Stir elderberries occasionally while simmering. Pour fruit into a jelly bag or several layers of damp cheesecloth which is placed over a large bowl. Let juice drip into a bowl. When dripping stops, press gently to remove final juice. Avoid hard pressing and your jelly will be clearer. Wash jars thoroughly and sterilize in boiling water while juice drips.

ELDERBERRY JELLY

3	cups elderberry juice
1/4	cup fresh lemon juice (2 lemons)
4 1/2	cups sugar
1	package fruit pectin
1/2	teaspoon butter or margarine

Measure juice *exactly*. If needed, you may add up to 1/2 cup water for the juice measure to be exact; be sure to use liquid measuring cups. Pour elderberry juice and lemon juice into an 8-quart saucepan. Measure sugar exactly (using dry measuring cups) into a separate bowl. Stir pectin into elderberry and lemon juice mixture. Add butter; this prevents foaming. Bring to a full rolling boil on high heat and stir constantly (a rolling boil cannot be stopped when stirring). Quickly add sugar and return to a *full rolling boil* and boil for exactly 1 minute; stir constantly. Remove from heat. Skim off foam and immediately fill jars and seal with flat lids and screw bands.

Tips: The secret of success with jellies and jams is exact measurement and timing. Be precise and have all ingredients and utensils ready.

Although elderberries are tiny and difficult to work with, you will find elderberry jelly an excellent accompaniment to a special game dinner.

Wild plums can also be used for a delicious, lovely jelly.

CHESTNUT DRESSING

1/2	cup butter or margarine
1	cup finely chopped celery
1	cup finely chopped onion
1	cup cooked, chopped, chestnuts (see tip)
6-8	cups cornbread crumbs (homemade is better)
1	egg, beaten
2	(or more) cups chicken broth
	Salt, pepper and sage to taste

Melt butter in skillet and sauté celery, onion and chestnuts. Cook slowly over low heat for 10 minutes; stir frequently as this burns easily. Add to cornbread crumbs in mixing bowl. Add beaten egg and broth; mix well. Dressing must be VERY moist; add more liquid if necessary. Season to taste with salt, pepper and sage. Bake in casserole dish at 350°F for 30 - 45 minutes or until golden brown.

Tip: To prepare chestnuts, cut an X on the round side of each chestnut with a sharp knife. Place in a saucepan, add water to cover and simmer chestnuts until they are tender (about 45 minutes). Shell and peel while warm. You can buy a nifty little inexpensive gadget for cutting the X in chestnuts that is safer and easier to use than a knife.

CHESTNUT SAUCE

3	tablespoons butter
3	tablespoons flour
1	cup milk
1/2	cup whipping cream
	Salt and freshly ground black pepper to taste
	Dash of nutmeg
1	cup cooked, finely chopped, chestnuts

Melt butter in saucepan. Add flour and stir constantly to cook flour. Add milk and cream; stir until thickened. Season with salt, pepper and nutmeg. Add chestnuts to sauce and heat through. Serve with venison or game birds.

Chestnut burrs in midsummer hold the promise of luscious nuts come autumn's time of ripening.

CHESTNUT SOUP

3	tablespoons butter
1/2	cup minced celery
1/2	cup grated carrots
1/2	cup minced onion
8	cups chicken broth
	Herb bouquet with 3 sprigs fresh parsley, 2 whole cloves, 1 bay leaf (wrapped in cheesecloth)
2	cups cooked, crumbled, chestnuts
1/4	cup Madeira wine
1/4	cup half-and-half
	Salt and freshly ground black pepper

A ripe chestnut ready to fall from its burr.

Melt butter in large saucepan. Add celery, carrots and onion and sauté until tender (about 10 minutes). Add chicken broth and herb bouquet. Bring to a boil, reduce heat, cover and simmer for 15 minutes. Add crumbled, cooked chestnuts and Madeira; simmer for about 5 minutes. Remove herb bag. Purée soup in batches with the steel blade of your food processor. Return soup to saucepan and add half-and-half. Season with salt and pepper. Heat over moderate heat, stirring constantly, until soup is hot. You may add more half-and-half if you like a thinner soup.

SERVES 6

Black Walnut and Banana Bread

BLACK WALNUT AND BANANA BREAD

1/2	cup vegetable oil
1	cup sugar
2	eggs
2	cups very ripe bananas, mashed with a fork
2	cups flour
1	teaspoon salt
1	teaspoon baking soda
1/2	cup finely chopped black walnuts

Mix vegetable oil, sugar, eggs and bananas well. Add flour, salt, baking soda and walnuts and mix until thoroughly blended. Place in greased loaf pan and bake at 350°F for 1 hour or in 4 small loaf pans for 40 minutes.

Tip: Small loaves are a nice addition to a fruit basket or hostess gift. Pecans are excellent in this bread if black walnuts are not available.

ICE CREAM PIE WITH BLACK WALNUT CRUST

1/2	cup finely chopped black walnuts
1	cup graham cracker crumbs
1/4	cup sugar
1/4	cup butter, softened
	Vanilla ice cream

Chop black walnuts very finely. Add graham cracker crumbs, sugar and butter. Mix well; press into pie plate. Bake at 375°F for about 8 minutes or until lightly browned. Cool. Spoon softened ice cream into pie shell. Place in the freezer. When served, top with a chocolate or berry sauce.

BLACK WALNUT POUND CAKE WITH FROSTING

1	cup butter (no substitute)
1/2	cup shortening
3	cups sugar
6	eggs
3	cups sifted flour
1	teaspoon baking powder
1 1/2	cups finely chopped black walnuts
1	teaspoon vanilla
1	cup half-and-half or milk

Cream butter and shortening thoroughly. Gradually add sugar; cream until light and fluffy. Add eggs one at a time, beating well after each. In a separate bowl, sift flour and baking powder and add chopped black walnuts to flour. In measuring cup, add vanilla to half-and-half. Add flour and walnut mixture alternately with half-and-half to creamed mixture. Blend and mix well. (Beating well is the secret to a pound cake.) Pour into a prepared 10-inch tube pan. Bake at 325°F for 1 hour and 15 - 25 minutes or until done. Cool for 10 minutes and remove from pan. Frost with Black Walnut Frosting.

BLACK WALNUT FROSTING

1	stick butter, melted
1	(16-ounce) box powdered sugar
	half-and-half or milk
1/4-1/2	cup finely chopped black walnuts

Blend melted butter and powdered sugar. Add enough half-and-half to reach desired consistency. Fold in walnuts and frost cooled cake.

NUTTING SECRETS

Locating edible nuts can provide quite a bit of family fun, and once you find productive trees, gathering the nuts can furnish you with their special treats year after year.

There are a number of secrets associated with nuts that will soon manifest themselves to the astute observer. Hazelnuts, for example, most frequently grow close to streams, while black walnuts prefer riverbottoms and fencerows. Hickories like ridgelines while chinquapins seem to fare particularly well in areas where there has been a hot fire within a decade or so.

Since a number of wild animals avidly seek nuts, you should expect some competition. When it comes to black walnuts, arguably the tastiest of all wild nuts, you can get a head start on squirrels by gathering them while they are still in the hull. Spread them out to dry in a sunny spot and remove the husks after they have lost all their moisture. Then dry the nuts a while longer before cracking. The meats will come out much easier, and the same is true of the shelling process for hickory nuts, butternuts and walnuts.

Once you have put in the arduous labor required to get a good supply of nutmeats, they will keep better when frozen. As an alternative, do what the pioneers did. Lay in a good supply and then shell the nuts as you need them. They will keep for a season while still in the shell.

Gathering nuts while they are still in the husk will give you a head start on squirrels. Let the nuts dry, remove the husks, and they are ready for the time-consuming process of shelling. Shown here: black walnuts.

BLACK WALNUT BARS

CRUST

1/2	cup butter
1/2	cup packed brown sugar
1	cup flour

FILLING

1	cup brown sugar
2	eggs, beaten
1/4	teaspoon salt
1	teaspoon vanilla
2	teaspoons flour
1/2	teaspoon baking powder
1 1/2	cups shredded coconut
1	cup chopped black walnuts

Cream butter and brown sugar. Slowly add flour and mix until crumbly. Pat into 7 x 11-inch baking dish. Bake for 8 - 10 minutes at 350°F until golden.

Combine brown sugar, eggs, salt and vanilla. In separate bowl, add flour and baking powder to coconut and walnuts. Blend into egg mixture and pour over baked crust. Return to oven and bake for an additional 15 - 20 minutes or until done. Cut into bars and place on wire racks to cool.

BLACK WALNUT VINAIGRETTE

1/4	cup chopped black walnuts
1/4	cup chopped English walnuts
	Salt to taste
1/4	cup vegetable oil
2	tablespoons olive oil
2	teaspoons wine vinegar
4	teaspoons freshly squeezed lemon juice
	Grated peel of 1 lemon
	Freshly ground black pepper

Toast nuts and cool. Briefly chop nuts in blender with salt. Do not chop nuts too finely; the nuts should be chunky. Add oils, vinegar, lemon juice, lemon peel and pepper; pulse to blend. Taste to adjust flavors. Serve over mixed green salad.

Tip: Toast nuts by placing in a dry non-stick skillet on medium-low heat and stir frequently until nuts are lightly browned.

CINNAMON OATMEAL COOKIES WITH BLACK WALNUTS

1/2	cup sugar
3/4	cup packed brown sugar
1 1/4	cup margarine
1	egg
1	teaspoon vanilla
3	cups oats, quick cooking or regular
1 1/2	cups flour
1 1/4	teaspoon cinnamon
1	teaspoon baking soda
1/2	teaspoon salt
1/2	cup raisins
2	cups black walnuts

Cream sugars and margarine; add egg and vanilla. Place dry ingredients in separate bowl and mix well. Add raisins and walnuts to dry ingredients. Combine creamed mixture and dry ingredients well. Drop by tablespoons onto cookie sheet. Bake at 350°F for 8 - 10 minutes or until golden brown.

YIELDS 3 DOZEN

Tip: Try chocolate chips in place of the raisins.

PECAN CURRIED FRUIT

1	(29-ounce) can sliced peaches
1	(15½-ounce) can pineapple chunks
1	(16-ounce) can pear halves
1	(16-ounce) can apricot halves
1	(16-ounce) jar maraschino cherries
½	cup chopped pecans
⅓	cup butter, melted
¾	cup packed light brown sugar
1	teaspoon - 1 tablespoon curry (amount depends on desired curry flavor)

Drain all fruits and arrange in 9 x 13-inch baking dish. Sprinkle with pecans. Combine butter, brown sugar and desired amount of curry powder. Top fruit with brown sugar mixture. Bake at 325°F for 45 minutes to an hour.

SERVES 8 - 10

Tip: This dish can be prepared using either mixtures or just one kind of fruit. This is delicious with quail and compliments other game dishes as well.

PECAN CRUNCH SWEET POTATOES

1	stick butter or margarine
2	eggs
2	teaspoons vanilla
1	cup sugar
3	cups cooked, mashed, sweet potatoes

Combine butter, eggs, vanilla and sugar. Add to mashed sweet potatoes. Place in baking dish.

TOPPING

⅓	stick butter, melted
1	cup packed brown sugar
2	tablespoons flour
1	cup finely chopped pecans

Mix topping ingredients and crumble over potatoes. Bake at 350°F for 25 - 30 minutes or until bubbly and golden brown.

BLACK WALNUT ICE CREAM

6	cups whole milk
1½	cups sugar
¼	cup flour
½	teaspoon salt
4	eggs, slightly beaten
1	tablespoon vanilla
½	pint whipping cream
1-1½	cups lightly toasted, chopped, black walnuts

Place milk in double boiler and heat. Mix sugar, flour and salt. Add enough hot milk to sugar mixture to make paste. Stir paste into hot milk. Cook until mixture thickens slightly. Add hot milk mixture gradually to eggs. Cook for about 2 minutes longer. Add vanilla. Cool quickly in refrigerator (overnight best). Whip cream slightly and add to custard along with chopped, toasted walnuts. Pour into ice cream churn and freeze by manufacturer's directions.

Pecan Curried Fruit

Pear and Hazelnut Salad

PEAR AND HAZELNUT SALAD

4-6 cups mixed greens (such as spinach, red leaf
         lettuce, Boston, bibb or romaine)
   2 large fresh pears, coarsely chopped (such as Bartlett,
         Bosc or Anjou)
   1 cup toasted, skinned, coarsely chopped hazelnuts
3-4 tablespoons mild blue cheese

Arrange lettuces on salad plates. Sprinkle
chopped pears, toasted hazelnuts and cheese on
each mound of lettuce. Drizzle with mild Italian
dressing or raspberry vinaigrette.

SERVES 4

Tip: Toast hazelnuts in a dry non-stick pan over medium heat until lightly browned. Stir frequently. While
nuts are still warm, place on a clean kitchen towel and
fold towel over onto top of nuts. Roll nuts with hands
on top of towel to loosen skins. Chop coarsely and add
to salad.

TOASTED PECANS

   4 cups pecan halves
1/3-1/2 cup butter, melted
   1/2 teaspoon salt or to taste

Place pecans in jelly roll pan. (Do not use dark
colored pan.) Drizzle butter over pecans. Stir
until nuts are well coated. Sprinkle pecans with
desired amount of salt. Bake at 325°F for 30 - 40
minutes or until lightly toasted. Stir frequently
(at least every 10 minutes) and watch carefully
to prevent pecans from getting too brown. Place
on paper towels to drain. Store in air tight containers.

Tips: These are ideal for teas, weddings, brunches, gift
baskets or cocktail parties.

For a change, try garlic salt.

PINE NUT OR HAZELNUT BUTTER

2 tablespoons pine nuts, toasted, or 2 tablespoons
*   hazelnuts, toasted and skinned*
4 tablespoons salted butter

Toast nuts in a dry non-stick skillet until golden brown. Stir or shake frequently. If you are using hazelnuts, place warm nuts on a kitchen towel, fold towel over top of nuts and roll nuts with hands on top of towel to loosen skins. Place either toasted pine nuts or toasted hazelnuts in food processor and pulse until nuts are finely chopped. Add butter and process until well blended and smooth. Nut butter can be added to rice, orzo, pasta, green beans, carrots, muffins, waffles, French toast or scones.

Tip: Nuts can be toasted on a baking sheet at 350°F until golden brown (about 5 - 8 minutes). Be sure to stir or shake frequently.

WILTED SPINACH WITH PINE NUTS

1 teaspoon olive oil
1½ tablespoons coarsely chopped pine nuts
1 pound spinach, stemmed, washed, torn and drained
1-2 tablespoons freshly grated Parmesan cheese

Heat olive oil in large skillet over medium-high heat. Add pine nuts and stir until golden (about 1 minute). Add spinach in batches if necessary and toss until just wilted (about 2 minutes). Season with salt and pepper. Sprinkle with Parmesan cheese and serve immediately.

SERVES 2

CHOCOLATE-DIPPED NUTS

1 (1-ounce) square semisweet chocolate
12 hazelnuts or pecans

Melt chocolate in a cup set into very hot, not boiling water. Dip nuts into chocolate, remove with fork and place on waxed paper. Refrigerate to harden chocolate. Serve with fruit and cheese for dessert, as a special appetizer or as a topping for vanilla ice cream.

NANCY'S CHRISTMAS FUDGE

1/2 pound butter (no substitute)
1 (13-ounce) can evaporated milk
5 cups sugar
2 (12-ounce) packages semisweet chocolate morsels
1 (7-ounce) jar marshmallow cream
1 teaspoon vanilla
1 cup chopped black walnuts
1 cup chopped California walnuts

Melt butter in a large saucepan and add milk. Stir to blend well, add sugar, stir constantly and bring to a boil. Boil vigorously for 8 minutes, stirring constantly; remove from heat. Add chocolate morsels and beat until chocolate is melted. Add marshmallow cream and beat until well blended and melted. Add vanilla and chopped nuts; blend well. Pour into 12 x 7 x 2-inch buttered, rectangular pan. Cool at least 6 hours before cutting into squares and store in air tight containers.

YIELDS 4 POUNDS

NUTTY SPREAD

1/2 cup butter, softened
3 ounces cream cheese, softened
1 cup finely chopped nuts (such as hickory nuts, hazelnuts, black walnuts or pecans)
1 tablespoons honey or to taste
1/4 teaspoon salt or to taste

Cream butter and cheese together. Add finely chopped nuts, honey and salt to taste. Serve as a spread for bagels, biscuits or crackers.

YIELDS 1 1/2 - 2 CUPS

GREEN BEANS WITH HAZELNUTS

1/2 cup hazelnuts
1/2 teaspoon salt
1 pound green beans, trimmed
4 tablespoons butter or margarine
1 garlic clove, minced
1/4 teaspoon freshly ground black pepper

Place hazelnuts in a dry skillet and toast on medium-low for about 10 minutes until lightly toasted. To remove skins, wrap hot hazelnuts in a cloth towel, roll hazelnuts with hands back and forth until skins come off. Remove skins; finely chop nuts.

In skillet, heat 1 inch water with salt to boiling. Add green beans, cover and reduce heat to low. Simmer, covered for 5 - 10 minutes until beans are tender-crisp. Remove and drain beans. In same skillet, melt margarine or butter over medium heat. Add garlic, hazelnuts and drained green beans. Sauté to cook garlic. Add pepper and adjust salt if necessary. Stir often and simmer until hot. Serve immediately.

SERVES 3 - 4

Tip: If you are unable to locate wild hazelnuts, a bigger version called filberts are grown commercially.

ORZO WITH HAZELNUTS

8 ounces orzo
¼ cup butter, softened
1 teaspoon lemon juice
¼ cup finely chopped hazelnuts
Salt to taste
Several dashes black pepper

Cook orzo according to package directions. Meanwhile, mix softened butter, lemon juice, hazelnuts, salt and pepper with a fork. Stir desired amount of butter into drained orzo and serve immediately.

Tip: Try this butter over green peas, other vegetables, fowl or salmon steaks.

HERBED RICE

2 tablespoons butter or margarine
½ cup chopped onion
¼-½ cup chopped hazelnuts
1 cup uncooked long-grain rice
2 cups chicken broth
½ cup chopped fresh parsley
½ teaspoon dried thyme
½ teaspoon dried marjoram
¼-¾ teaspoon curry powder (start on light side; add more to taste)
Dash of black pepper
Dash of paprika

Melt butter in skillet. Stir in onion, hazelnuts and rice. Sauté until onions are tender and nuts and rice are golden. Stir in broth, parsley, thyme, marjoram, curry powder, pepper and paprika. Mix well. Bring to a boil, reduce heat, cover and cook until liquid is absorbed and rice is tender. Taste and add more curry powder if desired.

HAZELNUT RICE

1/4 cup onion, minced
1 garlic clove, minced
1/2 cup uncooked white rice
1/2 cup chopped hazelnuts
3 tablespoons butter or margarine, melted
1 cup partially cooked wild rice (wild rice takes
      longer to cook and needs to be partially cooked
      before adding)
1/2 teaspoon celery seed
2 cups chicken broth
1 teaspoon lemon juice

Sauté onion, garlic, white rice and hazelnuts in
butter until onion is clear. Add pre-cooked wild
rice, celery seed, chicken broth and lemon juice.
Cover and reduce heat. Simmer until white rice
is tender and all liquid is absorbed.

<u>SERVES 4</u>

Tip: Serve with lemon garlic doves.

*A bowl of morel mushrooms holds the promise of some
heavenly dining.*

CREAMY MOREL TARTS

  Prepared pastry
2 cups fresh sliced mushrooms
2 tablespoons chopped green onions
2 tablespoons butter
2 tablespoons flour
1 cup light cream
2 tablespoons freshly grated Parmesan cheese
  Salt and freshly ground pepper
  Freshly grated nutmeg
  Minced parsley

Line 8 tart shells with pastry and bake at 450°F
for 8 - 10 minutes or until golden. In skillet,
sauté mushrooms and onions in butter until
tender (about 5 minutes). Remove onions and
mushrooms and set aside. Stir flour into drippings and cook for 1 minute. Add cream,
Parmesan cheese and seasonings to taste. Stir
constantly. When well-blended, return the
mushrooms to the skillet and cook until thickened; do not boil. Spoon into tart shells and
sprinkle with fresh parsley. Serve immediately.

Tip: Use puff pastry shells if you prefer.

CLAM STUFFED MORELS

10 medium to large fresh morel mushrooms, sliced in
      half lengthwise
1/3 cup butter or margarine, melted
1 clove garlic, minced
1 (6 1/2-ounce) can minced clams
3 tablespoons finely chopped green onions
1 tablespoon finely chopped fresh parsley
  Salt and pepper to taste
3/4 cup mayonnaise
1/2 tablespoon prepared mustard

Clean mushrooms well and remove stems. Cut
morels in half lengthwise. Chop stems finely.
Melt butter, add minced garlic and mushroom
stems and sauté for 8 - 10 minutes until stems
are tender. Drain clams and add to skillet with
onions, parsley and salt and pepper to taste.
Sauté for 5 minutes. Stuff morel halves with clam
mixture and place in a greased baking dish.
Combine mayonnaise and mustard and top each
stuffed morel half with a dollop. Bake for
10 - 15 minutes at 350°F. Serve immediately.

WILD MUSHROOM CHOWDER

2 cups fresh wild mushrooms, cleaned and sliced
1/4 cup chopped onions
1 cup peeled, diced, potatoes
1/2 cup finely chopped celery
1/2 cup finely chopped carrots
4 tablespoons butter
2 tablespoons olive oil
1 tablespoon flour
2 tablespoons cold water
2 cups chicken broth
1/2 teaspoon salt
1/2 teaspoon black pepper
1 cup milk
1/4 cup freshly grated Parmesan cheese

Clean and slice mushrooms; chop vegetables. Melt butter and add olive oil. Add onions and sauté until tender. Add mushrooms, potatoes, celery and carrots; cover and cook on medium heat for 15 - 20 minutes or until the vegetables are tender. In small bowl, thoroughly combine flour with cold water and slowly stir into vegetables. Add chicken broth, salt and pepper until heated through. Add milk and Parmesan cheese and heat; do not boil. Serve immediately topped with additional Parmesan cheese and paprika.

<u>SERVES 4</u>

Tip: You must be fond of mushrooms to enjoy this chowder. If you prefer a smooth soup, purée in the blender.

WILD MUSHROOM SAUCE

¼ cup butter
½ pound wild mushrooms, cleaned, sliced
¾ cup beef broth
1 tablespoon cornstarch
¼ cup white wine, such as Sauterne
   Salt and freshly ground black pepper

In 9-inch skillet, melt butter over medium heat.
Sauté mushrooms for about 5 minutes or until
tender. Stir in beef broth and heat to boiling.
Blend cornstarch into wine and gradually stir
into mushroom mixture. Cook until thickened;
stir constantly. Add salt and black pepper to taste.
Serve over venison steaks or roasts, burgers,
turkey patties, roasted turkey, green beans or
green peas.

SERVES 8

Tip: You will find this mushroom sauce quite versatile.

PARMESAN GRILLED PORTOBELLOS

4 whole portobello mushrooms, cleaned and stemmed
1 cup Italian salad dressing
   Freshly grated Parmesan cheese

Marinate mushrooms in dressing for 3 - 4 hours.
Turn often. (A sealable bag works well for marinating.) Drain mushrooms and grill until tender,
about 2 - 3 minutes per side. Sprinkle with freshly grated Parmesan cheese after grilling.

Tips: For a delicious portobello sandwich, place
Parmesan grilled portobellos on a toasted Kaiser roll
with a bit of pesto sauce, grilled or sautéed onions, lettuce and tomato.

For blue cheese portobellos, marinate as above, grill
mushroom on one side and turn, sprinkle with fresh
herbs of your choice (thyme, basil, oregano or chives),
crumble blue cheese and continue grilling until mushrooms are tender and cheese has partially melted.

PORTOBELLO SALAD

8-12 *slices portobello mushrooms, ³⁄4-inch thick*
½-1 *cup Italian salad dressing*
 1 *pound mixed salad greens or mesclun mix*
 ½ *cup roasted cashews*
 1 *yellow bell pepper, seeded and cut into thin slices*
 2 *tomatoes, sliced*
 1 *sweet onion, cut into rings*
 ½ *cup crumbled feta cheese*
   Balsamic vinaigrette or Italian dressing
   (desired amount)

Place mushrooms and Italian dressing in sealable plastic bag and marinate for 2 hours. Grill mushrooms for about 2 minutes per side. Cool slightly.

Place greens onto 4 salad plates; top with cashews, yellow peppers, tomatoes, onion, feta cheese and grilled mushrooms. Drizzle with dressing and serve immediately.

WATERCRESS SALAD WITH PARMESAN MUSTARD DRESSING

6-8 *cups fresh watercress*

Wash watercress and remove stems, if desired, and place in a salad bowl. Toss with desired amount of Parmesan Mustard Dressing. Garnish with a sprinkling of freshly grated Parmesan cheese. Serve immediately.

PARMESAN MUSTARD DRESSING

½ *cup Hellman's mayonnaise (or a very good quality*
   mayonnaise)
¼ *cup milk*
¼ *cup freshly grated Parmesan cheese*
 2 *tablespoons Dijonnaise cream mustard blend*
 2 *tablespoons freshly squeezed lemon juice*
¼ *teaspoon freshly ground black pepper*

Place all ingredients in small bowl and mix well with small wire whisk or fork. Cover and refrigerate until ready to serve.

<u>SERVES 6 - 8</u>

Tip: Dressing will keep for about a week in the refrigerator. Sometimes we mix mustards and use part Dijonnaise and part Dijon or brown mustard. This dressing is also great on a Caesar salad.

DANDELION GREENS

4	cups dandelion greens
1	small onion, chopped
1	garlic clove, minced
½	cup finely diced ham
2	tablespoons olive oil
2	teaspoons lemon juice
	Salt and pepper to taste

Boil greens 2 minutes and drain well. Sauté onion, garlic and ham in olive oil until onion is tender. Add boiled greens along with lemon juice, salt and pepper. Serve immediately.

BUTTERED SPRING GREENS

4	cups any wild spring greens
2	tablespoons butter or margarine
	Salt and pepper to taste

Sauté wild greens in skillet with melted butter until tender. Season with salt and pepper; garnish with hard-boiled egg slices, bacon bits, or green onions, or flavor with a splash of vinegar.

Ripe muscadine grapes—these grow widely across the South and are a delicacy cherished not only by man but by wild animals such as deer, fox and raccoons.

WILD WINES AND CORDIALS

All sorts of delicate, delightful alcoholic drinks can be made from foods that grow in the wild. Anyone with the proper equipment and some experience in winemaking at home can produce lovely wines and cordials. In the former case you don't even have to trouble with the process of fermentation.

A simple infusion of crushed berries and sugar (raspberries are a personal favorite) into vodka will produce as flavorful a cordial as one could want. Many kinds of wild berries lend themselves to winemaking, with raspberries, blackberries, dewberries and elderberries being particularly noteworthy. Dandelion blooms and the delicate blossoms of the elderberry also furnish the basic ingredients for light, fragrant wines. In addition to these, wild grapes such as scuppernongs, muscadines and fox grapes can be turned into robust wines which meld nicely with venison or into sweeter, after-dinner type drinks.

POKE SALAD

2-3 bunches tender poke sprouts
2 slices bacon, chopped
1 green onion, chopped
Salt and pepper to taste
Tabasco

Wash poke sprouts and chop. Parboil at least twice and drain. Fry chopped bacon and onion until light brown. Pour over greens and simmer for 10 - 15 minutes. Add salt and pepper. Serve with a dash of Tabasco. Garnish with chopped, boiled eggs.

Tip: The white roots and woody purple stalk of the mature pokeberry plant are poisonous, but the young, tender sprouts are a treat.

"KILT" RAMPS AND BRANCH LETTUCE

2-3 bacon slices
6-8 ramps
Tender branch lettuce (saxifrage) leaves

Fry the bacon until crisp and remove from the skillet. Slice the ramps lengthwise and sauté in the bacon grease. Crumble the bacon bits and sprinkle over the lettuce and cooked ramps.

SERVES 1

Tip: Ramps are a member of the leek family and grow widely in higher elevations up and down the spine of the Appalachian range. Though mild tasting, they have a powerful and lingering effect on the breath which makes garlic seem mild by comparison. Indeed, the recommended place to savor this springtime dish is on a back country camping trip of three or four days' duration.

WILTED DANDELION SALAD

4 cups very young, tender dandelion leaves, washed and drained well
1/4 cup chopped chives
5 slices bacon
1 tablespoon brown sugar
3 tablespoons vinegar
1 tablespoons water
1/4 teaspoon dry mustard
1/4 teaspoon salt
1/4 teaspoon black pepper
1 hard-cooked egg, chopped

Place washed greens on paper towels and pat dry. Combine greens with chives and place in a salad bowl. Fry bacon crisp and drain on a paper towel. Cool bacon grease slightly. Add brown sugar, vinegar, water, dry mustard, salt and pepper to bacon drippings in skillet. Mix well. Pour over dandelion greens and chives. Top with crumbled bacon and chopped egg; serve immediately.

SERVES 4 - 6

ETAH'S ARTICHOKE RELISH

4	quarts chopped vegetables including any of the following: Jerusalem artichokes, onion, cabbage, celery, green tomatoes, red or green bell pepper, cauliflower
1/2	cup salt
1/2	cup flour
2 1/2	cups sugar
1	(2-ounce) can dry mustard
1	tablespoon tumeric
1	tablespoon celery seed
1	tablespoon mustard seeds (optional)
1	quart vinegar

Prepare and chop vegetables; cover with salt and let set while you prepare flour paste. You may use any mixture of vegetables but have at least 1/4 Jerusalem artichokes and 1/4 green tomatoes; measure accurately and have a total of 4 quarts. The bell peppers and cauliflower are optional. Mix flour, sugar and spices. Add vinegar. Heat to boiling and cook until thick. Squeeze water out of vegetables (salt makes water come out of the vegetables) and add to paste mixture. Bring to a boil and simmer for 15 - 20 minutes; stir frequently to prevent sticking and scorching. When thickened, place in sterile jars and seal.

Tip: Try this relish on venison burgers, hot dogs, greens, poke salad or dry beans.

SASSAFRAS TEA

6	sassafras roots, 3 inches long
2-3	quarts water
	Sugar to taste

Wash dry roots well and place in a saucepan. Add 2 - 3 quarts of water, bring to a boil and simmer for 5 minutes or until tea is dark in color. Sweeten if desired and pour into mugs or cool and serve over ice in tall glasses.

Tip: Keep sassafras roots; they can be reused for several days. The flavor increases as the roots are used. Dig sassafras roots when the sap is down.

THE MAGIC OF MINT

Various types of mint grow wild across wide areas of the country. Crushed leaves from the plant can add delightful freshness to tea, lemonade and other drinks. Similarly, mint juleps—a heady and heavenly blend of crushed mint, sugar, bourbon and ice—epitomize the genteel Southern way of life at its best, but can be enjoyed anywhere a libation at the end of a hot day seems in order.

INDEX